Appetizers

APPETIZERS

Editorial Director
DONALD D. WOLF

Design and Layout
MARGOT L. WOLF

Published by
LEXICON PUBLICATIONS, INC.
387 Park Avenue South, New York, NY 10016

Cover illustration:
Fish Fondue, 66

Opposite title page:
Shrimp and Avocado Salad, 71

Copyright © 1987 by
Advance Publishers
1146 Solana Avenue
Winter Park, Florida 32789

ISBN: 0-7172-4525-X

Contents

Introduction, 7
Canapés, Sandwiches, and Loaves, 8
Spreads, Butters, and Dips, 17
Hot Finger Foods, 25
Mixed Appetizer Trays, 33
Molds, Mousses, and Pâtés, 36
Fish and Shellfish Appetizers, 46
Poultry and Meat Appetizer, 56
Vegetable Appetizers, 60
Fondues, Pies, and Rarebits, 66
Salads, 71
Cold Soups, 73
Appetizers from the Microwave Oven, 75
Index, 79

1 Gourmet Gouda Spread, 18
2 Peekaboo Appetizers, 27
3 Cheddar - Sausage Rolls, 56
4 Avocado Rye Rounds, 14
5 Scallops, 27
6 Rémoulade with Scallops, 27

APPETIZERS

Small, dainty, tempting to the eye and teasing to the palate, appetizers are artful little contrivances for putting company in a company mood. Such at least is their purpose. But they are so delicious and charming in their almost infinite variety that it is sometimes difficult to remember that it is the obligation of hostess and guest alike to maintain a sensible restraint where appetizers are concerned.

PLANNING APPETIZERS—There is no limit to the kinds of meat, poultry, fish, cheese, vegetables and fruits that can be used. Though imagination and ingenuity are the only limiting factors in selecting appetizers, there is one rule that should be followed—*Do not repeat any food in the main part of the meal that has been used in* *the appetizers.* Remember they are a part of the whole menu; select them to harmonize with the rest of the meal. Choose them for complementary flavors, for contrast in texture and color and variety of shape. Picture the serving dishes, trays and other appointments as you plan the menu.

Avoid a last-minute rush by wise selection (do not include too many appetizers that require last-minute doing), by careful buying and beforehand preparation.

Take cues from assembly-line production techniques for organizing your work. For example, use large sandwich loaves, cut in lengthwise slices, for canapé bases and finger sandwiches; stack several slices together and cut several identical shapes at one time; spread canapé bases all at one time.

Canapés, Sandwiches, and Loaves

Canapé Suggestions

Place sliced smoked salmon or turkey on toast rounds, garnish with white grapes and mayonnaise.

Spread toast rounds with Egg Butter. Cover with sliced smoked ham. Garnish with sliced stuffed olives.

Place thinly sliced tongue on toast rounds. Spread with tomato purée and garnish with olive slice.

Mix 3 ounces caviar with 4 teaspoons minced onion. Spread on toast rounds and garnish with cream cheese or strips of pimiento.

Cook 8 cleaned cooked shrimp in 2 tablespoons butter. Add ¼ teaspoon curry powder, ⅛ teaspoon dry mustard, 1 teaspoon sherry wine. Serve hot on small bread croustades or packaged appetizer shells.

Spread toast fingers with prepared mustard and top with whole sardines marinated in lemon juice.

Spread toast with butter, then with cream cheese. Garnish with strips of pimiento or sprinkle with sieved pimiento. Spread crackers with mayonnaise, cover with thin slices of cucumber and garnish with rosettes of snappy cheese spread and sprigs of parsley.

Spread bread fingers with cream cheese or with equal parts of Roquefort and cream cheese. Top with walnut meats.

Spread toast triangles with Egg Butter, then with pickled beets pressed through ricer. Sprinkle with a few drops of French dressing and garnish with sieved egg yolks.

Spread rounds of whole-wheat bread with Mustard Butter. Top with slice of tomato and sprinkle with salt. Or spread with Chive Butter and top tomato with slice of cucumber and a dash of paprika.

Make tomato aspic, adding minced cucumber and minced celery. Chill in ½-inch layer and cut into rounds. Serve on crackers.

Spread toast generously with thick mayonnaise. Dip into minced watercress and sprinkle with salt. Garnish with minced hard-cooked egg white.

Shrimp Canapés

SERVES 8

8 cooked jumbo shrimp split
   from head to tail
½ cup French dressing
16 toast rounds
4 tablespoons lemon
   mayonnaise
1½ ounces caviar
Parsley

1. Marinate shrimp in French dressing for 1 hour.
2. Spread toast rounds with lemon mayonnaise.
3. Place shrimp, flat side down, on toast.
4. Fill curve formed by shrimp with caviar.
5. Garnish with tiny sprig of parsley at the head of shrimp.

Wine-Cheese Canapés

ABOUT
24 CANAPÉS

½ cup whipped unsalted
   butter
4 teaspoons Roquefort cheese
4 toasted bread rounds
2 packages (3 ounces each)
   cream cheese
2 tablespoons sauterne
Parsley, minced
Pimento-stuffed olive slices
Paprika
Clear Glaze (below)

1. Whip together butter and Roquefort cheese. Spread onto toasted bread rounds.
2. Whip cream cheese with sauterne.
3. Pipe a swirl of the mixture onto each canapé. Roll edges in minced parsley. Top with pimento-stuffed olive slice; sprinkle.
4. Glaze and chill.

Clear Glaze: Soften **1 envelope unflavored gelatin** in ⅔ **cup cold water** in a bowl. Pour **1 cup boiling water** over softened gelatin and stir until gelatin is dissolved. Chill until slightly thickened. To glaze canapés: Place canapés on wire racks over a large shallow pan. Working quickly, spoon about 2 teaspoons of slightly thickened gelatin over each canapé. (Have ready a bowl of ice and water and a bowl of hot water. The gelatin may have to be set over one or the other during glazing to maintain the proper consistency.) The gelatin should cling slightly to canapés when spooned over them. Any drips may be scooped up and reused.

Curried Cheese Canapés

MAKES
30 CANAPÉS

½ lb. sharp Cheddar cheese
2 tablespoons butter
½ teaspoon curry powder
1 teaspoon grated onion
Madeira wine
Crisp crackers

1. Grind or grate the cheese and blend with softened butter, curry powder, onion and enough wine to make of spreading consistency.
2. Spread on crackers or Melba toast rounds and top each with a cocktail onion.

Sardine Canapés

MAKES
ABOUT 36

1 can (3¾ oz.) sardines
2 tablespoons mayonnaise
1 teaspoon catchup
1 teaspoon prepared
   horseradish
¼ teaspoon salt
¼ teaspoon paprika
Dash Worcestershire sauce
Crackers, Melba toast or
   toast rounds

1. Drain and mash sardines.
2. Combine with other ingredients except crackers and mix to a spreading consistency.
3. Spoon 1 teaspoon of mixture onto each cracker.

Tomato-and-Egg Canapés

MAKES
8 CANAPÉS

8 rounds bread
2 tablespoons mayonnaise
Sliced tomatoes
Hard-cooked eggs, sliced
Salt
4 stuffed green olives, sliced

1. Toast rounds of bread on one side and spread the untoasted side with mayonnaise.
2. Add thin slices of tomato, then slices of hard-cooked egg.
3. Sprinkle very lightly with salt and garnish with a slice or two of stuffed olives.

Olive Canapés

1 CUP

1 pound Greek olives, pitted
2 tablespoons olive oil
4 hard-cooked eggs, mashed
Pinch dry mustard
1 clove garlic, crushed in a
  garlic press
Pepper to taste
Egg yolks, hard-cooked and
  chopped for garnish
Scallions (green part),
  minced for garnish

1. Put olives and olive oil into a blender; purée. Blend in remaining ingredients except yolks and scallions.
2. Serve on **crackers,** or mound in a dish and serve crackers separately. Garnish with egg yolks and scallions.

Marrow Canapés

12 TO 15
PIECES

8 large marrow bones, cut in
  2-inch pieces
Salted water
½ cup butter
1 loaf cocktail-size black
  bread, cut in thick slices
¼ cup minced parsley
Ground red pepper

1. Using a thin sharp knife, loosen marrow from bones and remove. Soak marrow in salted water for 24 hours. Drain.
2. Cut marrow into ½-inch-thick rounds and poach in simmering water until tender (2 to 3 minutes). Remove with a slotted spoon. Drain on paper towels.
3. Melt butter in a skillet. Fry slices of bread on both sides.
4. Spread slices with marrow. Sprinkle with parsley and red pepper.
5. Place under broiler for a moment. Serve hot.

Half-and-Half Canapés

MAKES
8 CANAPÉS

½ cup flaked cooked salmon
2 tablespoons mayonnaise
1½ tablespoons lemon juice
¼ teaspoon salt
Dash pepper
8 toast rounds
3 tablespoons softened butter
½ cup mashed avocado
8 strips pimiento

1. Mix salmon, mayonnaise, ½ tablespoon lemon juice, salt and pepper.
2. Spread toast rounds with softened butter.
3. Spread half of each round with salmon mixture, the other half with avocado mixed with remaining lemon juice.
4. Mark the division with a pimiento strip.

Daisy Canapés

MAKES
8 CANAPÉS

8 rounds bread
⅓ cup softened butter
1½ ounces anchovy paste
4 hard-cooked eggs

1. Spread untoasted rounds of bread with butter and then with anchovy paste.
2. Cut narrow strips out of hard-cooked egg whites.
3. Arrange in petal fashion on paste and place sieved hard-cooked egg yolk in center.

Peppery Peanut Butter
and Coconut Sandwiches (below),
Shrimp Paste à la Creole (page 21)

Peppery Peanut Butter and Coconut Sandwiches

2 DOZEN
APPETIZERS

8 slices white bread
6 tablespoons peanut butter
2 tablespoons butter,
   softened
1 teaspoon Tabasco
½ cup fresh grated or
   chopped flaked coconut

1. Remove crusts from bread. Flatten each slice with a rolling pin and cut into 3 strips.
2. Combine peanut butter, butter, and Tabasco.
3. Spread peanut butter mixture on bread; dip in coconut. Roll each bread strip to form a pinwheel.
4. Chill thoroughly before serving.

Tuna in a Cucumber

1 can (7 oz.) tuna
1 pkg. (3 oz.) cream cheese
1 tablespoon mayonnaise
1 tablespoon lemon juice
½ teaspoon salt
¼ teaspoon pepper
1 tablespoon pickle relish
3 small cucumbers

1. Thoroughly blend first 7 ingredients together. Chill.
2. Core the cucumbers to remove centers.
3. Stuff tuna mixture into cavities and chill.
4. Slice and serve on assorted crackers.

Tomato Sandwich Hors d'Oeuvres

SERVES 8

8 tablespoons deviled ham
3 tablespoons mayonnaise
½ teaspoon minced onion
4 large tomatoes
Parsley

1. Combine the ham, mayonnaise and onion.
2. Rinse, dry and cut each tomato into four ¼-inch crosswise slices.
3. Spread deviled ham mixture on half the tomato slices and top each with a second tomato slice to make sandwiches.
4. Garnish with mayonnaise and a sprig of parsley and serve as a first course.

Avocado Sandwiches on Sour Dough

8 SERVINGS

2 avocados, thinly sliced and salted
¼ cup butter (½ stick), softened
½ teaspoon oregano leaves
¼ teaspoon each chervil, parsley flakes, and grated lemon peel
Dash onion powder
8 slices sour dough or Italian bread, diagonally cut

1. Prepare avocado slices.
2. Cream butter with seasonings. Spread thinly over bread.
3. Top with avocado slices. Serve with white wine.

Hawaiian Sandwiches

SERVES 6

1 cup minced, cooked chicken
½ cup moist, shredded coconut
¼ cup salad dressing
2 tablespoons finely chopped celery
½ teaspoon lemon juice
½ teaspoon salt
6 frankfurter buns, cut in halves

1. Combine the filling ingredients and blend well.
2. Spread between halves of buns.

Mosaic Sandwiches

MAKES
16 SANDWICHES

16 slices white bread
16 slices brown bread
Any desired canape spread or canape butter

1. Slice bread ¼ inch thick.
2. Cut into fancy shapes: hearts, diamonds, spades or clubs, and spread half of them with desired filling.
3. With a smaller cutter cut out the center of remaining pieces in the same shape as the original. For example, if the original shape was a heart, cut a heart shape out of center.
4. Insert white heart into brown bread and brown heart into white bread.
5. Place each on corresponding shape spread with filling.

Chicken-Mushroom Sandwiches

SERVES 6

1 cup minced cooked chicken
½ cup (4-oz. can) mushrooms, chopped
¼ cup salted almonds, chopped
3 tablespoons salad dressing
2 tablespoons chopped green olives
¼ teaspoon salt
⅛ teaspoon paprika
6 frankfurter buns, cut in halves

1. Combine the filling ingredients and blend well.
2. Spread between halves of buns.

Avocado Sandwiches on Sour Dough

Avocado Rye Rounds

ABOUT
2 DOZEN
APPETIZERS

½ cup cottage cheese
½ avocado, peeled and cut
  in pieces
1 tablespoon grated fresh
  onion
2 teaspoons fresh lemon juice
½ teaspoon Worcestershire
  sauce
3 drops Tabasco
¾ cup chopped cooked
  chicken
¼ cup chopped celery
Party rye bread slices,
  toasted and buttered
Pimento

1. Put cottage cheese and avocado into an electric blender or a bowl and blend or beat until fairly smooth. Blend in onion, lemon juice, Worcestershire sauce, and Tabasco. Stir in chicken and celery. Cover; chill several hours or overnight.
2. To serve, spread about 1 tablespoon avocado mixture on each rye toast slice. Garnish with pimento.

Crab Meat in Rolls

SERVES 8

8 finger rolls
1½ cups flaked crab meat
1½ cups diced celery
2 hard-cooked eggs, chopped
½ teaspoon salt
¼ teaspoon pepper
Dash Tabasco sauce
3 tablespoons lemon juice
½ cup salad dressing

1. Make a lengthwise cut in center of top of each roll, spread apart and remove soft part.
2. Mix crabmeat, celery, eggs, salt, pepper, Tabasco sauce, lemon juice and salad dressing together and fill center of rolls.
3. Place rolls on crisp lettuce to serve.

Olive Pinwheels

MAKES
6 TO 8
PINWHEELS

6 tablespoons ground boiled
  ham
2 tablespoons mayonnaise
1 teaspoon horseradish
1 loaf sandwich bread
4 tablespoons butter
6 stuffed olives

1. Combine ham, mayonnaise and horseradish.
2. Remove all crusts from bread.
3. Cut a ¼-inch lengthwise slice from bread.
4. Spread with softened butter and with ham mixture.
5. Place olives in a line crosswise at one end of the bread; roll bread starting at the end of slice.
6. Wrap in plastic wrap or waxed paper; chill for several hours.
7. When ready to serve, cut crosswise into slices any thickness desired.

Crisp Cheese Crackers

ABOUT
3 DOZEN

¼ cup sesame seed
2 cups all-purpose flour
Salt (optional)
½ teaspoon ground red
  pepper
1½ cups grated kefalotyri
  cheese
¾ cup butter, softened
¼ cup olive oil
2 egg yolks, beaten, for
  brushing
Sesame seed

1. Combine ¼ cup sesame seed, flour, salt, red pepper, and cheese. Work in butter and oil, using hands. Mix until dough holds together.
2. Roll dough out on lightly floured board. Cut into small diamond shapes. Transfer to cookie sheets. Brush with egg.
3. Bake at 350°F about 12 minutes, or until golden.

Crusty Roll Tempters

SERVES 6

6 crusty rolls
1 cup chopped cooked ham
1 cup finely shredded
  cabbage
2 hard-cooked eggs, chopped
¼ cup chopped green pepper
¼ cup pimiento strips
½ cup chopped salted
  peanuts
2 tablespoons chopped
  pickled onion
¼ cup mayonnaise
¾ teaspoon salt
¼ teaspoon pepper

1. Cut rolls lengthwise through center; scoop out centers to within ¼ inch of crust.
2. Butter inside if desired.
3. Mix remaining ingredients together.
4. Fill the lower halves of rolls generously with ham mixture.
5. Place scooped-out upper section of rolls over filling; cut into halves.

Yule Sandwich Log

Prepare sandwich fillings: – Deviled ham – peanut butter; egg-bacon; avocado-pineapple; and cheese shrimp. Prepare cranberry-cheese frosting. Remove crusts from unsliced sandwich loaf and cut lengthwise into 5 slices. Butter 4 slices of bread and spread each with one of the 4 fillings, reserving the cranberry-cheese mixture for top and sides of loaf. Stack the 4 slices and top with the remaining slice of bread. Press loaf firmly together and wrap in plastic wrap. Chill in refrigerator 1 hour. Frost loaf with cranberry-cheese mixture, making lengthwise ridges with a spatula. Garnish platter with cinnamon pear halves placed on lettuce leaves, using maraschino cherries for "bell clappers."

Deviled Ham – Peanut Butter Filling: Combine ⅓ cup peanut butter with 1 can (3 oz.) deviled ham, ¼ cup salad dressing and 3 tablespoons chopped dill pickle.
MAKES ¾ CUP

Egg Bacon Filling: Combine 2 hard-cooked eggs, chopped, ⅓ cup crumbled cooked bacon and 3 tablespoons salad dressing.
MAKES ¾ CUP

Avocado-Pineapple Filling: Combine ⅓ cup mashed avocado, 2 tablespoons drained, crushed pineapple, 1 teaspoon lemon juice, 1 tablespoon salad dressing and dash salt.
MAKES ½ CUP

Cheese-Shrimp Filling: Combine ½ cup pimiento cream cheese, ½ teaspoon chili sauce, ⅓ cup finely chopped shrimp and ½ teaspoon lemon juice.
MAKES ⅔ CUP

Cranberry-Cheese Frosting: Combine 3 packages (3 oz. each) cream cheese and ⅓ cup strained cranberry sauce. Beat with electric beater until smooth and fluffy.
MAKES 1¾ CUP

Ham Loaf en Brioche

Brioche Dough:
1 package (13¾ ounces) hot
 roll mix
¼ cup warm water
⅓ cup milk
⅓ cup butter or margarine
2 tablespoons sugar
3 eggs, beaten

Ham Loaf:
2 cups ground cooked ham
1 pound ground veal or lean
 beef

2 eggs, beaten
2 cups fine soft bread
 crumbs
¾ cup California Sauterne
½ teaspoon dry mustard
½ teaspoon salt
¼ teaspoon pepper
½ cup coarsely chopped ripe
 olives
¼ cup diced pimento
1 tablespoon instant minced
 onion

1. For brioche dough, combine yeast from packet in hot roll mix with warm water.
2. Scald milk and cool to lukewarm.
3. Cream butter and sugar. Add eggs and yeast; mix well. Stir in flour mixture from mix alternately with milk, beating until smooth after each addition. Cover tightly; let rise in a warm place until light (about 1 hour). Stir down and set in refrigerator until thoroughly chilled.
4. Meanwhile, prepare ham loaf.
5. For ham loaf, combine all ingredients and mix well. Turn into a greased fluted brioche pan, about 8½ inches across top and about 1-quart capacity; pack into pan and round up center.
6. Bake at 350°F 1 hour. Cool in pan about 10 minutes, then turn out of pan and cool thoroughly.

7. Divide chilled brioche dough in half. Roll each portion into a round about 10 inches in diameter. Turn cooled ham loaf upside down and fit a round of dough over bottom and sides. Trim off excess dough. Holding dough in place, quickly invert loaf and fit other round of dough over top and sides. Trim edges evenly.
8. Place dough-wrapped loaf in a well-greased brioche pan a size larger than one used for ham loaf, about 9½ inches in diameter across top and about 2-quarts capacity.
9. Shape dough trimmings into a ball and place on top of loaf. Let rise in a warm place about 30 to 45 minutes, or until dough is light.
10. Set on lowest shelf of 375°F oven. Bake 10 to 15 minutes, or until top is browned. Place a piece of brown paper or aluminum foil over top of loaf. Continue baking about 25 minutes, or until nicely browned and baked through (test brioche with wooden pick).
11. Turn loaf out of pan and serve warm or cold, cut in wedges.
ABOUT 8 SERVINGS

Spreads, Butters, Dips

Nippy Beef Spread

1½ CUPS
SPREAD

1 package (3 ounces)
vacuum-packed wafer-sliced
beef, finely chopped
1 package (8 ounces) cream
cheese (at room
temperature)
2 tablespoons prepared
horseradish
1 teaspoon Worcestershire
sauce
Dinner crêpes (below)

Combine ingredients for spread. Serve with Wafer Crêpes.
(below)

Note: Spread can be stored in a covered container in the
refrigerator for 1 week, or it can be frozen.

Wafer Crêpes

ABOUT
8 DOZEN
WAFERS

2½ cups crepe batter (below)
Cooking oil

1. Heat a skillet or griddle over medium heat, and brush
with oil.
2. Pour ½ tablespoon batter in skillet, but do not swirl the
pan. Pour 3 or 4 more crêpes, turn when brown, and brown
on other side. Place crêpes on ungreased baking sheet.
3. Bake at 350°F about 15 minutes, turning over halfway
through baking. Remove from baking sheet and serve with
dips, spreads, or cheese.

Dinner Crêpes

ABOUT
18 CRÊPES

1 cup all-purpose flour
⅛ teaspoon salt
3 eggs
1½ cups milk
2 tablespoons melted butter or
oil

1. Sift flour and salt. Add eggs, one at a time, beating
thoroughly. Gradually add milk, mixing until blended. Add
melted butter or oil and beat until smooth. (Or mix in an
electric blender until smooth.)
2. Let batter stand for 1 hour before cooking crêpes.

Party Spread

MAKES
ABOUT 1⅓
CUPS

1 pkg. (8 oz.) cream cheese
¼ cup butter, softened
1 teaspoon paprika
¼ teaspoon dry mustard
½ teaspoon onion salt
1½ teaspoons caraway seeds
2 teaspoons capers, drained
1 teaspoon prepared mustard
2 teaspoons minced onion

1. Blend cream cheese and butter together.
2. Blend in remaining ingredients and chill several hours to
blend flavors.
3. Spread on thinly sliced pumpernickel or rye bread or
crackers.

Gourmet Gouda Spread (Pictured on page 7)

ABOUT
1 CUP
CHEESE SPREAD

1 round baby Gouda cheese
(8 to 10 ounces) at room
temperature
3 tablespoons blue cheese
2 tablespoons dry white
wine
2 tablespoons butter
1 teaspoon prepared mustard
¼ teaspoon Worcestershire
sauce

1. Cut top off Gouda cheese through red wax. Scoop out cheese, leaving a ¼-inch shell. Refrigerate shell.
2. Combine Gouda and blue cheese in a small bowl; mix in wine, butter, mustard, and Worcestershire sauce. Fill shell with cheese mixture. Chill several hours or overnight.
3. Before serving, bring to room temperature. Accompany with crackers or party rye bread slices.

Sardine Spread

MAKES 1 CUP

½ cup butter or margarine,
softened
1 can (3½ oz.) sardines
1 tablespoon lemon juice
⅛ teaspoon paprika

1. Cream the softened butter.
2. Remove skins from sardines and mash sardines with lemon juice and paprika.
3. Beat into the butter.

Shrimp Spread

⅔ CUPS
SPREAD FOR
ABOUT
7 DOZEN
CRACKERS
OR TINY
CREAM PUFFS

½ cup butter or margarine,
softened
2 green onions with some
tops
2 parsley sprigs
¼ teaspoon salt
⅛ teaspoon garlic powder
Dash pepper
1 package (12 ounces) frozen
cooked shrimp, thawed
½ cup beer
1 tablespoon capers
(optional)
Fancy crackers or tiny
cream puffs

1. Using a food processor or blender, process butter, onions, parsley, and seasonings until vegetables are minced and mixture is smooth. (With blender, prepare in 2 or 3 batches.)
2. Add shrimp, beer, and capers. Process to a smooth paste.
3. Serve at room temperature on crackers or in tiny cream puffs. Use a rounded teaspoon for each. One half recipe of Shrimp Spread fills one recipe Appetizer Puffs (below).

Appetizer Puffs

ABOUT
40 PUFFS

1 cup beer
½ cup butter or margarine
½ teaspoon salt
1 cup all-purpose flour
4 eggs

1. Heat beer, butter, and salt to boiling in a saucepan.
2. Add flour at once. Beat vigorously with a wooden spoon until mixture leaves sides of pan and forms a smooth ball.
3. Add eggs, one at a time, beating until smooth.
4. Drop mixture by rounded teaspoonfuls onto a greased cookie sheet, 1 inch apart.
5. Bake at 450°F 10 minutes. Turn oven control to 350°F and bake 5 to 10 minutes more, or until lightly browned and puffed.
6. Cool. Split and fill with desired filling.

Hot Crab Spread

1 package (8 ounces) cream cheese, softened
1 tablespoon milk
2 teaspoons Worcestershire sauce
1 can (7½ ounces) Alaska King crab, drained and flaked, or 1 package (6 ounces) frozen crab meat, thawed, drained, and flaked
2 tablespoons chopped green onion
2 tablespoons toasted slivered almonds

1. Combine cream cheese, milk, Worcestershire sauce, crab, and green onion. Place in small individual casseroles. Sprinkle with almonds.
2. Bake, uncovered, at 350°F 15 minutes. Serve with **assorted crackers.**

2 CUPS

Chicken Liver Spread

ABOUT
4 CUPS

½ pound chicken livers
1 cup milk
¼ cup rendered chicken fat
  or margarine
1 medium onion, cut in
  quarters
3 hard-cooked eggs, peeled
  and cut in half
½ pound cooked ham or
  cooked fresh pork, cut up
¼ teaspoon salt
¼ teaspoon pepper
⅛ teaspoon garlic powder
  (optional)

1. Soak livers in milk 2 hours. Drain livers and discard milk.
2. Melt fat in skillet. Add livers and onion and cook over medium heat until tender.
3. Combine livers, pan drippings, and all remaining ingredients. Grind or mince.
4. Add extra melted chicken fat or margarine, if desired, to make spread of desired spreading consistency.

Liver-Bologna Spread

MAKES
1½ CUPS

¼ pound liverwurst sausage,
  mashed
¼ pound bologna, chopped
  fine
1 hard-cooked egg, chopped
  fine
1 sweet pickle, chopped fine
¼ teaspoon dry mustard
1 tablespoon lemon juice
Mayonnaise to moisten

Combine all ingredients in a bowl with enough mayonnaise to moisten to spreading consistency.

Spring Cottage Cheese Spread

ABOUT
2⅓ CUPS

1 carton (12 to 14 ounces)
  cottage cheese
½ cup sour cream
8 radishes, shredded
3 tablespoons sliced green
  onion
½ teaspoon salt
Lettuce leaves
Radish roses
Rye or French bread

1. Mix cottage cheese with sour cream. Add radishes, onion, and salt; toss to mix well.
2. Mound on lettuce leaves. Garnish with radish roses. Surround with bread.

Eggplant Appetizer

ABOUT
4 CUPS

1 large eggplant
1 medium onion, minced
1 garlic clove, crushed in a
  garlic press
1 teaspoon chopped parsley
½ teaspoon freshly dried
  mint
½ cup olive oil
1 tablespoon wine vinegar
  (or more to taste)
Juice of 1 large lemon
Salt and pepper to taste

1. To prepare eggplant, place in a baking pan and prick top in four or five places with a fork.
2. Bake at 350°F about 45 minutes, or until skin is wrinkled and the surface is soft.
3. Cool eggplant slightly and cut in half. Scoop out the flesh and place in a blender. Add onion, garlic, parsley, and mint. Blend until well mixed.
4. Combine olive oil, vinegar, and lemon juice. Add to the eggplant mixture and blend well. Season with salt and pepper.
5. Chill. Serve with **toasted French** or **pita bread.** May also be used as a dip for fresh vegetables, or served separately as a first course.

Shrimp Paste à la Creole (Pictured on page 11)

Fresh shrimp
Court Bouillon for Fish and
   Shellfish (below)
¼ cup butter, melted
1 garlic clove, crushed in a
   garlic press
⅛ teaspoon ground mace
⅛ teaspoon pepper
Tabasco to taste

1. Cook enough shrimp in bouillon to make 4 cups shelled shrimp.
2. Put shrimp, hot melted garlic, mace, pepper, and Tabasco into container of an electric blender; process 10 seconds.
3. Serve on **toasted cassava** or **Melba toast.**

Court Bouillon for Fish and Shellfish

ABOUT
1 QUART

1 onion
1 leek
1 carrot
3 celery stalks
5 parsley sprigs
1 basil sprig
2 tablespoons olive oil
2 quarts boiling water
Bouquet garni
6 peppercorns, cracked
2 whole cloves
6 dried Italian pepper pods
   or 1 whole pink hot pepper
½ cup amber rum

1. Finely chop fresh vegetables and herbs together.
2. Heat oil in a large saucepan, add chopped mixture, and cook until lightly browned. Add boiling water, bouquet garni, peppercorns, cloves, pepper pods, and rum. Cover; boil 30 minutes. Boil uncovered to reduce volume by half.
3. Strain and cool before using.

Guacamole

ABOUT
2 CUPS DIP

1 small clove garlic
2 large ripe avocados, peeled
2 tablespoons lemon juice
1 teaspoon chili powder
   (optional)
Salt to taste

1. Using **steel blade,** mince garlic. Add avocado and remaining ingredients and process to desired consistency. (Remember to use quick on/off motions if a coarse, chunky consistency is desired.)
2. Serve as a dip with tortilla chips, on lettuce as a salad, or as a filling for tacos.

Note: If not served immediately, refrigerate in a covered bowl with avocado pits immersed in guacamole. This will help prevent the avocado from darkening on standing.

Guacamole

Canapé Butters

All these butters are prepared as follows: Cream butter thoroughly. Grind fish, meat, or vegetables to a paste and combine with the seasoning and butter. If mixture is not entirely smooth, rub through a sieve. Spread on toast rounds and garnish appropriately or use as a base for sandwich fillings.

Pimiento Butter

½ cup butter
¼ cup mashed pimiento
2 teaspoons India relish, drained

Ham Butter

½ cup butter
¼ pound cooked ham
2 hard-cooked eggs, chopped
Dash pepper

Egg Butter

½ cup butter
4 hard-cooked egg yolks
Few grains cayenne
6 drops Worcestershire sauce

Cheese Butter

½ cup butter
¼ cup grated Parmesan cheese or 1½ ounces Roquefort or ½ cup snappy cheese spread

Olive Butter

¼ cup butter
2 tablespoons chopped olives
¼ teaspoon lemon juice

Shrimp Butter

1 cup butter
1 cup minced cooked shrimp
¼ teaspoon salt
Dash paprika
1 tablespoon lemon juice

Dried Beef Butter

½ cup butter
3-4 ounces dried beef
Few drops Tabasco sauce

Horseradish Butter

½ cup butter
¼ cup grated horseradish

Chili Butter

¼ cup butter
2 tablespoons chili sauce, drained

Anchovy Butter

1 cup butter
½ cup minced anchovies or 4 tablespoons anchovy paste
2 teaspoons lemon juice
4 drops onion juice

Variations:
Substitute herring, bloaters, crawfish, lobster, smoked salmon, whitefish or sardines for the anchovies.

Mustard Butter

1 CUP

½ cup butter (at room temperature)
½ cup prepared mustard

1. Beat the butter with the mustard until creamy.
2. Spread on toast rounds to serve with **sardines or herring.**

Onion-Chive Butter

ABOUT ⅔ CUP

1 tablespoon sliced green onion
1 tablespoon snipped chives
½ cup butter (at room temperature)

1. Blend onion, chives, and butter.
2. Form into a roll about 1 inch in diameter. Chill.
3. Cut into small disks.

Creamy
Shrimp
Dip

Creamy Shrimp Dip

ABOUT
2½ CUPS DIP

1 package (8 ounces) cream
cheese, softened
1 can (10¾ ounces) con-
densed cream of shrimp
soup
2 tablespoons chopped green
onion
1 teaspoon lemon juice
¼ teaspoon curry powder
Dash garlic powder
4 drops Tabasco
Raw vegetables

1. Combine cream cheese, soup, green onion, lemon juice,
curry powder, garlic powder, and Tabasco with a beater just
until blended; do not overbeat. Chill.
2. Serve as a dip with raw vegetable pieces.

Creamy Corn Dip

ABOUT
6 SERVINGS

2 tablespooons butter or
margarine
2 tablespoons finely chopped
green pepper
¼ cup flour
¼ teaspoon salt
⅛ teaspoon cayenne pepper
1½ cups chicken broth
(dissolve 1 chicken bouillon
cube in 1½ cups
boiling water)
4 ounces Swiss cheese,
shredded (about 1 cup)
1 can (8 ounces) cream-style
corn
4 drops Tabasco
Party rye bread, buttered
and toasted, or crusty
French bread cubes

1. Heat butter in cooking pan of a chafing dish over medium
heat. Add green pepper and cook until just tender, occasionally moving and turning with a spoon. Blend in flour,
salt, and cayenne. Heat until mixture bubbles, stirring
constantly.
2. Blend in chicken broth, cooking and stirring until sauce
thickens.
3. Remove from heat. Add cheese all at one time, stirring
until cheese is melted. Stir in corn and Tabasco.
4. Keep warm over hot water while serving.

Blue Cheese in a Melon

½ pound blue cheese
1 pkg. (8 oz.) cream cheese
¼ cup heavy cream
1 ripe cantaloupe

1. Thoroughly blend the blue and cream cheese together;
beat in the cream until fluffy.
2. Using a melon-ball cutter, scoop melon balls from ripe
cantaloupe.
3. Spoon cheese dip into cantaloupe shell.
4. Serve with assorted crackers and melon balls on cocktail
picks.

Chili con Queso Dip

3¼ CUPS DIP

1 cup chopped onion
2 cans (4 ounces each) green chilies, chopped and drained
2 large cloves garlic, mashed
2 tablespoons cooking oil
1 pound process sharp Cheddar cheese, cut into chunks
1 teaspoon Worcestershire sauce
¼ teaspoon paprika
¼ teaspoon salt
½ cup tomato juice

1. Sauté onion, green chilies, and garlic in oil in cooking pan of chafing dish over medium heat until onion is tender.
2. Reduce heat to low, and add remaining ingredients, except tomato juice. Cook, stirring constantly, until cheese is melted.
3. Add tomato juice gradually until dip is the desired consistency. Place over hot water to keep warm.
4. Serve with **corn chips.**

Tangy Cheese Dip

ABOUT 2 CUPS

4 ounces Muenster cheese or other semisoft cheese, finely shredded (1 cup)
3 ounces blue cheese, crumbled
1 package (3 ounces) cream cheese, softened
⅛ teaspoon garlic powder
¾ cup beer (about)

1. After shredding, let Muenster cheese stand at room temperature at least 1 hour.
2. Using an electric blender or food processor, blend cheeses and garlic. Gradually add enough beer to make a mixture of dipping consistency.
3. Serve at room temperature with crackers for dipping.

Hot Finger Foods

Feta Cheese Triangles

ABOUT
100 PIECES

1 pound feta cheese,
  crumbled
2 egg yolks
1 whole egg
3 tablespoons chopped
  parsley
Dash finely ground pepper
¾ pound butter, melted and
  kept warm
1 pound filo

1. Mash feta cheese with a fork. Add egg yolks, egg, parsley, and pepper.
2. Melt butter in a saucepan. Keep warm, but do not allow to brown.
3. Lay a sheet of filo on a large cutting board. Brush with melted butter. Cut into strips about 1½ to 2 inches wide. Place ½ teaspoon of the cheese mixture on each strip about 1 inch from base. Fold to form a triangle. Continue until all cheese mixture and filo have been used.
4. Place triangles, side by side, in a shallow roasting pan or baking sheet.*
5. Bake at 350°F about 20 minutes, or until golden brown. Serve at once.

Note: Feta cheese triangles freeze well. Before serving, remove from freezer and let stand 15 to 20 minutes. Bake at 325°F until golden brown.

*Pan must have four joined sides; otherwise butter will fall to bottom of the oven and burn.

Fried Cheese

Kefalotyri or kasseri cheese,
sliced lengthwise in ¼-inch-
thick wedges (about 1
pound for 4 people)
2 egg yolks minced with 2
tablespoons water
Flour
Olive oil
2 lemons, cut in quarters

1. Dip cheese slices into egg-yolk mixture, then into flour, coating each side evenly. Shake off excess flour.
2. In a 10-inch skillet, heat a ¼-inch layer of olive oil. When the oil begins to smoke, add the cheese. Fry first on one side, then on the other.
3. Remove from skillet and squeeze some lemon juice on each slice. Serve immediately. Allow 2 slices for each person.

Crab Meat Quiche

16 APPETIZERS

1 unbaked 9-inch pie shell
2 eggs
1 cup half-and-half
½ teaspoon salt
Dash ground red pepper
¾ cup (3 ounces) shredded
Gruyère cheese
1 tablespoon flour
1 can (7½ ounces) Alaska
King crab, drained and
flaked

1. Prick bottom and sides of pie shell. Bake at 450°F 10 minutes, or until delicately browned.
2. Beat together eggs, half-and-half, salt, and red pepper.
3. Combine cheeses, flour, and crab; sprinkle evenly in pie shell. Pour in egg mixture.
4. Bake, uncovered, at 325°F 45 minutes, or until tip of knife inserted 1 inch from center comes out clean. Let stand a few minutes. Cut into wedges to serve.

Clam and Walnut Stuffed Mushrooms

20 large mushrooms
½ cup butter or margarine
1 clove garlic, minced
1 can (10 ounces) minced or
whole baby clams, drained
1 cup soft bread crumbs

½ cup chopped walnuts
¼ cup chopped parsley
¼ teaspoon salt
¼ teaspoon black pepper
Walnut halves (optional)
Parsley sprigs (optional)

1. Rinse mushrooms and pat dry. Remove stems and chop (about 1 cup); set aside.
2. Melt butter in a large skillet. Use about 3 tablespoons of melted butter to brush on mushroom caps. Place caps in a shallow pan.
3. To butter remaining in skillet, add garlic and reserved chopped mushroom stems; sauté 2 minutes. Add clams, bread crumbs, nuts, parsley, salt, and pepper; mix well.
4. Spoon stuffing into mushroom caps, piling high.
5. Bake at 350°F about 12 minutes, or until hot.
6. If desired, garnish with walnut halves and parsley sprigs.
20 STUFFED MUSHROOMS

Puff Shrimp with Orange Ginger Sauce

40 TO 50 APPETIZERS

Orange Ginger Sauce (see recipe)
Fat for deep frying heated to 375° F
2 pounds medium raw shrimp (20 to 25 per pound)
3 egg yolks
1/2 cup white wine
3/4 cup all-purpose flour
1 teaspoon salt
1/4 teaspoon pepper
3 egg whites

Orange Ginger Sauce:
1 cup orange marmalade
2 tablespoons soy sauce
1/4 cup sherry
1 piece whole ginger root
1 clove garlic, minced

1. Prepare and cool Orange Ginger Sauce.
2. Fill a deep saucepan or automatic deep fryer one-half to two-thirds full with fat for deep frying; heat slowly to 375°F.
3. Shell and devein raw shrimp and set aside.
4. Beat together in a bowl egg yolks, wine, flour, salt, and pepper until smooth.
5. Beat egg white until stiff, not dry, peaks are formed. Fold egg whites into egg yolk mixture.
6. Dry shrimp thoroughly and dip into batter, coating well.
7. Deep-fry one layer deep in heated fat 2 to 3 minutes on each side, or until golden brown. Remove from fat with a slotted spoon. Drain on absorbent paper. Be sure temperature of fat is 375°F before frying each layer. Serve shrimp hot accompanied with the Orange Ginger Sauce for dipping.
8. For Orange Ginger Sauce, combine in a saucepan marmalade, soy sauce, sherry, ginger root, and minced garlic. Stir over low heat until mixture bubbles. Remove from heat. Cool. Remove ginger before serving.

Rémoulade with Scallops

ABOUT 1 CUP SAUCE

1 cup sour cream
1 1/2 teaspoons prepared mustard
1 1/2 teaspoons chopped capers
1 1/2 teaspoons parsley flakes
1 teaspoon snipped chives
1 small clove garlic, crushed in a garlic press
Butter
1 package (12 ounces) frozen scallops, thawed and drained

1. Turn sour cream into a bowl. Gently blend in mustard, capers, parsley flakes, chives, and garlic. Cover and chill several hours or overnight.
2. Heat desired amount of butter in a skillet, add scallops, and sauté about 5 minutes, or until lightly browned. Serve on wooden picks with the sauce.

Peekaboo Appetizers

54 APPETIZERS

1 can (7 3/4 ounces) salmon, drained and flaked
1/3 cup sour cream
1/3 cup finely chopped green pepper
2 tablespoons finely chopped onion
1/4 teaspoon dill weed
1/4 teaspoon salt
3 sticks pie crust mix
1/2 cup sour cream
Toasted sesame seed

1. Combine salmon, 1/3 cup sour cream, green pepper, onion, dill weed, and salt in a bowl.
2. Meanwhile, prepare pastry according to package directions. Form into 3 balls; roll each into a 12x6-inch rectangle and cut into 18 squares. Place about 1 teaspoon filling in center of each square; bring corners together over filling and press pastry edges together. Place on a buttered baking sheet.
3. Bake at 450°F 12 minutes, or until lightly browned.
4. To serve, spoon about 1/2 teaspoon sour cream on each appetizer and top with sesame seed. Serve hot or cold.

Empanadas

24 TO 30
EMPANADAS

Picadillo:
½ **pound coarsely chopped beef**
½ **pound coarsely chopped pork**
½ **cup chopped onion**
1 **small clove garlic, minced**
½ **cup chopped raw apple**
¾ **cup chopped canned tomatoes**
¼ **cup raisins**
¾ **teaspoon salt**
⅛ **teaspoon pepper**
Dash ground cinnamon
Dash ground cloves
¼ **cup chopped almonds**

Pastry:
4 **cups all-purpose flour**
1¼ **teaspoons salt**
1⅓ **cups lard or shortening**
⅔ **cup icy cold water (about)**

1. For picadillo, cook beef and pork together in large skillet until well browned. Add onion and garlic and cook until onion is soft. Add remaining ingredients, except almonds, and simmer 15 to 20 minutes longer until flavors are well blended.
2. Stir in almonds. Cool.
3. For pastry, mix flour and salt in a bowl. Cut in lard until mixture resembles coarse crumbs. Sprinkle water over flour mixture, stirring lightly with a fork until all dry ingredients hold together. Divide dough in four portions.
4. On a lightly floured surface, roll one portion of dough at a time to ⅛-inch thickness.
5. Using a 5-inch cardboard circle as a pattern, cut rounds of pastry with a knife. Place a rounded spoonful of filling in center of each round. Fold one side over filling to meet opposite side. Seal by dampening inside edges of pastry and pressing together with tines of fork.
6. Place empanadas on a baking sheet. Bake at 400°F 15 to 20 minutes, or until lightly browned. Or fry in **fat for deep frying** heated to 365°F until browned (about 3 minutes); turn once.

Cocktail Meatballs

30 to 40
MEATBALLS

1 **large onion, minced**
2 **tablespoons olive oil**
1½ **pounds freshly ground round steak (half each of lamb and veal)**
3 **tablespoons cracker meal**
2 **cups firm-type bread, crust removed**
2 **eggs**
6 **tablespoons chopped parsley**
2 **teaspoons oregano, crushed**
1½ **teaspoons mint**
2 **tablespoons vinegar**
Salt and pepper to taste
Flour
Olive or corn oil for deep frying heated to 365°F

1. Brown half of onion in 2 tablespoons oil in a small frying pan. Mix with the uncooked onion and add to meat in a large bowl. Add the remaining ingredients except flour and oil. Toss lightly with two forks to mix thoroughly.
2. Dust hands with flour. Roll a small amount of meat at a time between palms, shaping into a ball.
3. To heated fat in deep fryer, add the meatballs a layer at a time. Fry until browned on all sides (about 12 minutes). Serve hot.

Cocktail Meatballs

Tangerine Yakatori

4 SERVINGS

½ cup tangerine or orange juice
¼ cup dry white wine
3 tablespoons light soy sauce
½ bunch green onions, cut in 1-inch pieces
2 large tangerines or oranges, peeled, sectioned, and seeded
2 large whole chicken breasts, skinned, boned, and cut in 1 x ¼-inch strips

1. Combine all ingredients in a mixing bowl. Refrigerate covered 2 hours, stirring occasionally. Drain; reserve marinade.
2. Thread ingredients alternately on wooden skewers. Broil 4 inches from heat until chicken is done (about 3 minutes on each side).
3. Heat marinade until bubbly. Serve in individual cups as a dipping sauce.

Fried Calf, Lamb, or Chicken Livers

4 SERVINGS

1 pound livers, cut in small pieces (do not cut chicken livers)
1½ cups flour, seasoned with pepper for dredging
Olive oil for frying
2 lemons, quartered
Salt to taste

1. Rinse livers in cool water. Drain on absorbent paper.
2. Dip livers in flour. Shake off excess.
3. In a deep skillet, heat olive oil to smoking. Brown livers on both sides over medium heat.
4. Squeeze lemon juice on each piece. Season with salt. Serve at once.

Barbecued Lamb Innards

10 TO 20 PIECES

1 large intestine
Innards (heart, liver, kidneys, lungs, and sweetbreads) from a milk-fed calf
Salt to taste
1 tablespoon vinegar
¾ cup olive oil
Juice of 2 to 3 lemons
2 garlic cloves, crushed in a garlic press
2 teaspoons pepper
2 teaspoons oregano
1 teaspoon thyme
2 lamb casings, washed and drained
Pepper to taste

1. Rinse intestine in lukewarm water. Using a long spit, turn inside out. Rub salt over surface. Wash thoroughly in lots of lukewarm water.
2. Put innards in a large bowl. Cover with lukewarm water. Add salt and vinegar. Let stand ½ hour. Drain. Discard membranes and connective tissues. Cut into pieces.
3. Combine olive oil, lemon juice, garlic, 2 teaspoons pepper, oregano, and thyme. Add innards. Marinate in refrigerator 4 to 6 hours, turning occasionally.
4. Drain innards, reserving marinade. Knot one end of casing, then stuff with innards and knot other end.
5. Put a skewer beside the filled casing. Tie to the skewer with the empty casing by turning the casing around the length of the skewer.
6. Charcoal-broil over embers heated until they are white, turning about every 10 minutes and brushing frequently with the marinade. Cook until tender (about 2½ hours). Remove from spit. Cut into 2-inch pieces. Sprinkle with pepper. Serve hot.

Chicken Fritters Guadeloupe

ABOUT
20 FRITTERS

2 cups minced cooked
chicken
3 tablespoons finely chopped
parsley
2 tablespoons finely chopped
chives
3 tablespoons fresh bread
crumbs
1 tablespoon grated onion
1 tablespoon curry powder
Salt to taste
¼ teaspoon cayenne or red
pepper
¼ cup Dijon mustard
½ cup dry bread crumbs
1 egg, beaten with 1 tea-
spoon peanut oil
Oil for frying, heated to
365°F

1. Mix chicken with parsley, chives, fresh bread crumbs, onion, and seasonings. Shape mixture into walnut-size balls, roll in dry bread crumbs, then in beaten egg, and again in bread crumbs. Chill in refrigerator.
2. Just before serving, fry in hot oil until golden brown. Drain on absorbent paper and serve hot.

Egg Rolls

ABOUT
15 EGG ROLLS

Skins:
1½ cups flour
½ teaspoon salt
2 eggs, fork beaten
1½ cups water

Filling:
¼ pound cooked roast pork,
cut in 1-inch cubes
6 medium shrimp, shelled
and cooked
3 green onions, trimmed and
cut in 1-inch pieces
½ cup water chestnuts,
drained
3 stalks celery, cut in 3-inch
pieces
4 to 6 leaves Chinese
cabbage
½ cup bean sprouts, drained
2 tablespoons peanut oil
1 tablespoon soy sauce
1 tablespoon sherry
½ teaspoon salt
½ teaspoon sugar

1. For skins, with **steel blade** of food processor in bowl, add flour and salt.
2. Combine lightly beaten eggs and water. With machine on, add liquid ingredients through the feed tube and process a few seconds until batter is smooth.
3. Lightly grease a 7- or 8-inch skillet with peanut oil and heat over medium heat until it smokes. Quickly pour exactly 2 tablespoons batter into the center of the pan and rotate to evenly spread the batter into a 5-inch circle. Cook about 2 minutes, until the edges of the pancake begin to curl. Remove to a plate and cover with a damp cloth. Repeat procedure until all batter is used, stacking skins on plate. If not using a well-seasoned pan, it will be necessary to lightly grease the skillet before making each skin.
4. Let skins cool completely before filling and rolling.
5. For filling, using **steel blade,** separately process pork and shrimp, using quick on/off motions, until coarsely chopped. Set aside.
6. Still using **steel blade,** process green onions until finely chopped. Set aside.
7. Using **shredding disc,** separately shred water chestnuts and celery, removing each from bowl; pack celery vertically in the feed tube, filling it as full as possible.
8. To slice Chinese cabbage, lightly roll together 2 to 3 leaves of cabbage and place vertically in feed tube. Slice with **slicing disc,** using light pressure.
9. Combine shredded celery, sliced Chinese cabbage, and bean sprouts in a bowl. These ingredients must be blanched before proceeding. To do so, cover with boiling water, stir a few times only, and remove to a colander. Immediately rinse with cold water and drain thoroughly. Roll ingredients in a towel to remove any excess moisture. Set aside.

10. Heat peanut oil in a wok. Add chopped pork and shrimp and stir-fry to heat through. Add remaining ingredients and stir-fry very briefly to heat through. Remove to a colander and let cool completely.

11. For rolls, skins and fillings must be completely cooled for successful egg rolls.

12. Place 2 to 3 tablespoons of filling slightly below the center of the skin. Fold the bottom side up to cover filling. Fold in sides and roll the skin. Brush the top edge with unbeaten egg white and seal like an envelope.

13. To cook, heat ¼-inch peanut oil in a large skillet and fry on both sides until lighly browned. Drain on paper towels.

Note: Egg rolls can be made in advance. To reheat, place in 325°F oven for 10 to 15 minutes.

Egg Rolls

Eggplant Fritters

18 FRITTERS

3 long thin eggplants
1 tablespoon lime juice
Salt, pepper, and cayenne or red pepper to taste
1½ cups all-purpose flour (about)
¾ cup beer (about)
Oil for deep frying heated to 365°F
Salt

1. Slice eggplants into eighteen ½-inch rounds. Season with lime juice, salt, and ground peppers. Marinate 15 minutes.

2. Make a batter the consistency of whipping cream by mixing flour with beer.

3. Dip and coat eggplant slices in batter. Fry in heated oil until golden brown. Drain on absorbent paper. Sprinkle lightly with salt. Serve hot.

Artichoke Fritters: Follow recipe for Eggplant Fritters. Substitute **artichoke hearts** or **bottoms** for eggplant rounds.

Corn Fritters

ABOUT 30 FRITTERS

1 cup fresh corn kernels
½ cup butter
1 cup all-purpose flour
4 eggs
Corn oil for frying, heated to 365°F

1. Cook corn until soft in boiling salted water in a saucepan; drain thoroughly, reserving 1 cup liquid. Melt butter with corn liquid in saucepan, add flour, and cook, stirring rapidly, until mixture is smooth and rolls away from the sides of pan.

2. Remove from heat and add the eggs, one at a time, beating well after each addition. Stir in cooked corn.

3. Drop batter by spoonfuls into heated oil and fry until golden and well puffed. Drain on absorbent paper. Serve hot.

Tomato Toast

16 APPETIZERS

¼ cup finely chopped onion
2 tablespoons butter or margarine
Italian-style tomatoes (canned), drained
1 teaspoon sugar
⅛ teaspoon salt
1 egg yolk, fork beaten
¼ to ½ teaspoon Worcestershire sauce
¼ cup shredded Parmesan cheese
4 slices white bread, toasted, crusts removed, and toast cut in quarters
Snipped fresh parsley or crushed dried basil or oregano

1. Add onion to heated butter in a heavy saucepan and cook until tender, stirring occasionally.
2. Force enough of the drained tomatoes through a sieve to yield 1½ cups. Add to onion with sugar and salt; cook, stirring occasionally, until liquid evaporates and mixture is thick (about 25 minutes).
3. Stir a small amount of tomato mixture into egg yolk; blend thoroughly and return to saucepan. Cook and stir 5 minutes.
4. Mix in Worcestershire sauce and half of cheese; spread generously on toast quarters. Sprinkle half of appetizers with the remaining cheese and half with the parsley.
5. Broil appetizers 3 to 4 inches from heat until bubbly. Serve hot.

Fresh Mushrooms in Sour Cream

ABOUT 2 CUPS

1 pound fresh mushrooms, sliced
⅔ cup sliced green onions with tops
2 tablespoons butter or margarine
1 tablespoon fresh lemon juice
1 tablespoon flour
1 cup sour cream
2 tablespoons chopped fresh dill or 1 tablespoon dill weed
¼ teaspoon salt
⅛ teaspoon pepper
Small rounds of rye or Melba toast

1. Sauté mushrooms and onions in butter and lemon juice for 4 minutes. Stir in flour. Cook slowly, stirring 1 minute. Add sour cream, dill, salt, and pepper. Cook and stir 1 minute.
2. Serve warm on toast.

Acra

20 FRITTERS

5 dried Italian pepper pods or 1 small piece hot pepper
1 tablespoon coarse salt
6 peppercorns
½ medium onion, chopped
2 garlic cloves
1 egg
1 cup finely grated malanga root*
Peanut oil for frying, heated to 365°F

1. In a mortar, pound together to a paste the pepper pods, salt, peppercorns, onion, and garlic.
2. Add seasoning paste and egg to grated malanga root; beat until light.
3. Drop mixture by spoonfuls into heated oil and fry until golden. Drain on absorbent paper.

*Malanga root can be found in Puerto Rican markets.

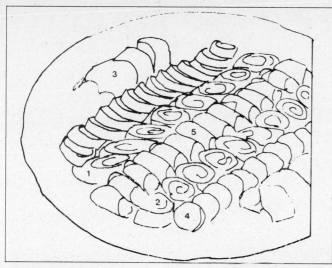

Mixed Appetizer Trays

Crêpe Appetizer Platter:
1 Chili Pinwheels, 35
2 Chili Turnovers, 35
3 Fried Cheese Roll, 35
4 Chili—Nut Log, 35
5 Cocktail Frank Wrap—Ups, 34

Fresh
Sweet
Cherry
Appetizer
Tray

Fresh Sweet Cherry Appetizer Tray

Fresh sweet cherries
Assorted cheeses (Cheddar,
  Swiss, Gouda, Kuminost)
Sweet gherkins, thickly sliced
  salami, thinly sliced
Cream cheese
Horseradish
Parsley

1. Wash cherries just before serving and put into a serving bowl.
2. Cut some of the Cheddar and Swiss cheeses into ½-inch cubes and put, along with sliced gherkins, onto party picks. Slice remaining cheeses.
3. Soften cream cheese at room temperature and season with a small amount of horseradish. Spread on salami slices and shape into cornucopias, fastening with wooden picks. Garnish with parsley.
4. Arrange all appetizers on a large tray with the cherries.

Cocktail Frank Wrap-Ups (Pictured on page 33)

16 APPETIZERS

2 dinner crêpes (page 17)
1 teaspoon prepared mustard
1 package (5½ ounces)
  cocktail frankfurters

1. Spread each crêpe on one side with ½ teaspoon mustard. Cut each crêpe in 8 wedges. Starting from wide edge, roll up a frankfurter in each wedge. Place seam side down in a shallow baking pan.
2. Bake at 375°F 10 minutes. Spear with wooden picks and serve with **bottled cocktail sauce.**

MIXED APPETIZER TRAYS • 35

Chili-Nut Log (Pictured on page 33)

3 LOGS

8 ounces process sharp
  Cheddar cheese spread (at
  room temperature)
2 tablespoons butter or
  margarine (at room
  temperature)
½ teaspoon minced onion
¼ teaspoon minced garlic
1 tablespoon chili powder
Dash cayenne pepper
2 tablespoons lemon juice
⅓ cup finely chopped
  walnuts or pecans
3 dinner crêpes (page 17)
Melted butter or margarine
2 tablespoons chopped
  parsley

1. Combine cheese, 2 tablespoons butter, onion, garlic, chili powder, cayenne, lemon juice, and nuts. Mix until well blended. Shape into 3 or 4 logs. (If mixture is too soft to work with, refrigerate for 10 to 15 minutes.)
2. Place log at one end of crêpe and roll up. Brush outside of crêpe with melted butter and roll in parsley. Refrigerate 10 minutes, slice, and serve with picks.
3. Store in refrigerator up to 1 week, or store in freezer.

Fried Cheese Roll (Pictured on page 33)

6 ROLLS

6 (1-ounce) wedges Gruyère
  cheese
6 dinner crêpes (page 17)
2 eggs, beaten
⅓ cup fine dry bread
  crumbs, seasoned or plain
Oil for frying heated to
  375°F

1. Coarsely shred 1 wedge of cheese over 1 crêpe to within 1 inch of crêpe edges. Fold two opposite sides of crêpe over 1 inch. Continue folding as directed in egg-roll method (below). Dip rolls into eggs. Coat thoroughly with bread crumbs.
2. Fry in 375°F oil until golden brown (about 5 minutes). Cool slightly. Cut into 1-inch pieces and serve.

Egg-Roll Method: Place filling in a line down the center of the crêpe, leaving enough space at either end of the filling to fold crêpe up and over the filling. Lift edge and tuck around and under filling. Roll up firmly.

Chili Pinwheels (Pictured on page 33)

8 ROLLS

1 can (about 15½ ounces)
  kidney beans
½ teaspoon chili powder
½ pound ground beef
⅓ cup chopped onion
¼ cup chopped green
  pepper
2 tablespoons ketchup
2 dashes Tabasco
Salt and pepper
8 dinner crepes (page 17)

1. Drain and mash beans. Blend in chili powder. Set aside.
2. Sauté beef with onion and green pepper. When onion and green pepper are tender, remove from heat and drain off any liquid. Stir ketchup, Tabasco, and bean mixture into drained meat. Season with salt and pepper to taste.
3. For bite-size snacks or hors d'oeuvres, assemble by jelly-roll method (below).
4. Bake at 375°F 15 minutes. Cool 5 minutes and slice.

Chili Turnovers: Follow recipe for Chili Pinwheels for filling. Assemble by turnover method (below). Bake at 375°F 15 minutes; serve hot. These can be picked up and eaten like a sandwich.

Jelly-Roll Method: Spread crêpe with filling according to recipe. Lift edge and fold under. Roll up firmly.

Turnover Method: Using a slotted spoon, place filling on one half of the crêpe leaving a ¼- to ½-inch border. Moisten the back of a spoon with sauce from the filling. Run moistened spoon along rim of crêpe. Fold crêpe in half and press along rim to seal.

Molds, Mousses, Pâtés

Mushroom Cheese Mold

2 packages (8 ounces each)
  cream cheese, softened
½ pound Cheddar cheese,
  shredded (about 2 cups)
1 clove garlic, crushed
1½ teaspoons brown
  mustard
¼ teaspoon salt
1 can (3 to 4 ounces)
  mushroom stems and
  pieces, drained and
  chopped
¼ cup finely chopped onion
2 tablespoons finely diced
  pimento
2 tablespoons finely chopped
  parsley
Sliced mushrooms (optional)
Parsley (optional)

1. Combine cheeses, garlic, mustard, and salt in a bowl. Add chopped mushrooms, onion, pimento, and parsley; mix well.
2. Turn mixture into a lightly buttered 3-cup mold. Refrigerate until firm.
3. Unmold onto serving platter. Garnish with sliced mushrooms and parsley, if desired. Serve with crackers.

Mustard Relish Mold

ABOUT
12 SERVINGS

1 cup cold water
2 envelopes unflavored
 gelatin
6 eggs
1½ cups sugar
1½ tablespoons dry mustard
1¼ teaspoons salt
1½ cups vinegar
1 16-ounce can peas (about
 1¾ cups, drained)
1 cup (about 2 medium-size)
 grated carrot
1 cup chopped celery
1 tablespoon minced parsley
Curly endive or other crisp
 greens

1. A 1½-quart mold will be needed.
2. Pour water into a small bowl.
3. Sprinkle gelatin evenly over cold water.
4. Let stand until softened.
5. Beat eggs slightly in top of a double boiler.
6. Blend in a mixture of sugar, mustard, and salt.
7. Add vinegar gradually, stirring constantly.
8. Cook over simmering water, stirring constantly, until mixture thickens. Remove from simmering water. Stir softened gelatin; add to egg mixture and stir until gelatin is completely dissolved. Cool, chill until mixture begins to gel (gets slightly thicker).
9. Meanwhile drain peas.
10. Lightly oil the mold with salad or cooking oil (not olive oil) and set it aside to drain.
11. Prepare carrot, celery, and parsley.
12. When gelatin is of desired consistency, blend in the vegetables. Turn into the prepared mold. Chill in refrigerator until firm.
13. Unmold onto chilled serving plate. Garnish with curly endive or other crisp greens.

German Beer Cheese

3 CUPS

½ pound Cheddar cheese
½ pound Swiss cheese
2 teaspoons Worcestershire
 sauce
1 teaspoon dry mustard
1 small garlic clove, mashed
½ cup beer (about)

1. Shred cheeses finely. Or put through a meat grinder, using finest blade.
2. Add Worcestershire sauce, dry mustard, garlic, and enough beer to make a mixture of spreading consistency.
3. Turn into a 3-cup rounded bowl or mold; pack firmly. Chill. Unmold and serve at room temperature with **small rye rounds** or **crackers.**

Tomato Aspic

6 TO 8
SERVINGS

4 cups tomato juice
⅓ cup chopped celery leaves
⅓ cup chopped onion
2½ tablespoons sugar
1¼ teaspoons salt
1 bay leaf
½ cup cold water
2 envelopes unflavored
 gelatin
2½ tablespoons cider vinegar

1. Set out a 1-quart mold.
2. Pour tomato juice into a saucepan.
3. Add celery leaves, onion, sugar, salt and bay leaf to tomato juice.
4. Simmer, uncovered 10 minutes, stirring occasionally.
5. Meanwhile, pour water into a small bowl.
6. Sprinkle gelatin evenly over water.
7. Let stand until softened.
8. Lightly oil the mold with salad or cooking oil (not olive oil); set aside to drain.
9. Remove tomato juice mixture from heat and strain into a large bowl. Immediately add the softened gelatin to hot tomato juice mixture and stir until gelatin is completely dissolved.
10. Add cider vinegar and stir well.
11. Pour tomato-juice mixture into the prepared mold. Cool; chill in refrigerator until firm.
12. Unmold onto chilled serving plate.

Beermato Aspic

Beermato Aspic

8 SERVINGS

1 can (18 ounces) tomato
  juice (2¼ cups)
1 can or bottle (12 ounces)
  beer
⅓ cup chopped onion
⅓ cup chopped celery leaves
  (optional)
2½ tablespoons sugar
1 tablespoon lemon juice
½ teaspoon salt
1 bay leaf
2 envelopes unflavored
  gelatin
¼ cup cold water

1. Combine tomato juice (reserve ¼ cup), beer, onion, celery leaves, sugar, lemon juice, salt, and bay leaf in a saucepan. Simmer, uncovered, 10 minutes.
2. Meanwhile, sprinkle gelatin over cold water and reserved tomato juice in a large bowl; let stand to soften.
3. Strain hot tomato juice mixture into bowl; stir until gelatin is completely dissolved.
4. Pour into a lightly oiled 1-quart mold. Chill until firm. Unmold onto crisp **salad greens.**

Note: For individual aspics, turn mixture into 8 oiled ½-cup molds. Chill until firm.

Feet in Aspic

8 SERVINGS

1½ pounds pigs' feet or calves' feet
½ pound lean pork or veal shanks
3 carrots, pared
1 onion, cut in quarters
2 stalks celery or 1 small celery root
2 bay leaves
5 peppercorns
3 whole allspice
2 cloves garlic, crushed (optional)
Water
1 tablespoon salt
½ cup chopped fresh parsley
⅓ cup vinegar
Lemon wedges
Parsley sprigs

1. Have the butcher skin and split pigs' feet.
2. Cook pigs feet, pork, vegetables, bay leaves, peppercorns, allspice, garlic, and water to cover in a covered saucepot 2 hours on low heat. Skim off foam and add salt, parsley, and vinegar; cook 2 hours.
3. Strain off the stock; set aside. Take out pigs' feet and carrots. Discard onion and spices. Dice meat and slice carrots.
4. Arrange sliced carrots on bottom of an oiled 2-quart mold. Put meat on top of carrots in mold. Add parsley. Pour stock into mold.
5. Chill until set, at least 4 hours. Skim off fat.
6. Unmold onto platter. Garnish with lemon wedges and parsley sprigs.

Jellied Mélange

SERVES 8

2 tablespoons unflavored gelatin
½ cup cold water
3¾ cups hot chicken broth
2 tablespoons onion juice
1 cup chopped cooked chicken
½ cup chopped cooked ham
½ cup chopped celery
1 pimiento, minced
Mayonnaise
Parsley

1. Soften gelatin in cold water for 5 minutes and dissolve in hot broth.
2. Add onion juice.
3. Cool; when mixture begins to thicken, stir in chicken, ham, celery and pimiento and pour into small molds. Chill.
4. Serve on lettuce garnished with mayonnaise and parsley.

Shrimp Melange: Omit ham, use tomato juice instead of chicken broth and chopped, cleaned cooked shrimp instead of chicken.

Fabulous Cheese Mousse

MAKES
1-PINT MOLD

¼ cup cold water
1 tablespoon unflavored gelatin
3 pkgs. (1¼ oz. each) Roquefort cheese
2 pkgs. (1⅓ oz. each) Camembert cheese
1 egg yolk, slightly beaten
1 tablespoon sherry
1 teaspoon Worcestershire sauce
1 egg white
½ cup heavy cream, whipped

1. Soften gelatin in the cold water; dissolve completely over low heat.
2. Force the cheeses through a fine sieve, then blend in the egg yolk, sherry and Worcestershire sauce.
3. Beat until smooth.
4. Add dissolved gelatin to cheese mixture and beat until smooth. (Cheeses and other ingredients may be mixed in electric blender if desired.)
5. Beat egg white until rounded peaks are formed; fold into cheese mixture along with the whipped cream.
6. Turn into a 1-pint fancy mold which has been rinsed with cold water.
7. Chill until firm and unmold on chilled serving plate.
8. Serve with crackers.

Chicken Mousse Amandine

8 SERVINGS

½ cup dry white wine, such as sauterne
2 envelopes unflavored gelatin
3 egg yolks
1 cup milk
1 cup chicken broth
½ cup (about 3 ounces) almonds, finely chopped
3 cups ground cooked chicken
¼ cup mayonnaise
2 tablespoons minced parsley
2 tablespoons chopped green olives
1 teaspoon lemon juice
1 teaspoon onion juice
½ teaspoon salt
½ teaspoon celery salt
Few grains paprika
Few grains cayenne pepper
½ cup chilled heavy cream
Sprigs of parsley

1. Place a small bowl and a rotary beater in refrigerator to chill.
2. Pour wine into a small cup and sprinkle gelatin evenly over wine; set aside.
3. Beat egg yolks slightly in top of a double boiler; add milk gradually, stirring constantly.
4. Stir in the chicken broth gradually. Cook over simmering water, stirring constantly and rapidly until mixture coats a metal spoon.
5. Remove from heat. Stir softened gelatin and immediately stir it into the hot mixture until gelatin is completely dissolved. Cool; chill in refrigerator or over ice and water until gelatin mixture begins to gel (becomes slightly thicker). If mixture is placed over ice and water, stir frequently; if placed in refrigerator, stir occasionally.
6. Blend almonds and chicken into chilled custard mixture along with mayonnaise, parsley, olives, lemon juice, onion juice, and a mixture of salt, celery salt, paprika, and cayenne pepper.
7. Using the chilled bowl and beater, beat cream until of medium consistency (piles softly).
8. Fold whipped cream into chicken mixture. Turn into a 1½-quart fancy mold. Chill in refrigerator until firm.
9. Unmold onto chilled serving plate and, if desired, garnish with sprigs of parsley.

Ham Mousse

SERVES 10

1 tablespoon gelatin
¼ cup cold water
1½ cups chicken stock
3 cups ham, chopped
¼ cup celery, chopped
1 tablespoon onion, grated
½ cup mayonnaise
¼ cup sweet-sour pickles, chopped
3 tablespoons dill
½ teaspoon white pepper

Garnish:
Watercress
2 sliced cucumbers
6 radishes

1. Place gelatin in ¼ cup water. Add chicken stock and bring to a boil.
2. Chill mixture. When it is almost set add rest of ingredients.
3. Moisten a mold with cold water and add mixture. Chill until firm.

Cheese Mousse

SERVES 4

¾ cup heavy cream
7 ounces cream cheese
1 package unflavored gelatin
½ teaspoon salt
½ teaspoon paprika
1 tablespoon chopped chives

1. Whip the heavy cream till stiff. Stir in the cream cheese until smooth and add half the cream to it.
2. Place the gelatin in 2 tablespoons water and dissolve over low heat. Stir the gelatin in the cream and cream cheese mixture and add the rest of the whipped cream. Add seasonings.
3. Pour the cheese cream into a water-rinsed ring mold. Place in refrigerature to set. Serve garnished with **watercress, cucumbers** and **radishes**.

Cheese Mousse

Individual Chicken Terrines

8 SERVINGS

½ cup thinly sliced small
  carrots
¼ cup brandy
2 pounds boned chicken,
  coarsely chopped
1 small onion
1 small carrot
1 teaspoon salt
¼ teaspoon nutmeg
1 egg, lightly beaten
2 teaspoons vegetable oil
2 tablespoons ice water
1½ tablespoons matzo meal
  or white cornmeal
Vegetable oil
Watercress
Cucumber Sauce, if desired
  (page 43)

1. Simmer carrot slices in brandy in a covered saucepan just until tender (about 3 minutes). Remove carrots with a slotted spoon; reserve. Mix a quarter of the chicken with brandy; remove from heat and let stand 45 minutes. Drain.
2. Mince remaining chicken, the onion, and carrot in a food processor or blender; remove to a mixing bowl. Stir in marinated chicken, salt, nutmeg, egg, oil, and ice water; mix well. Sprinkle matzo meal over mixture; mix well.
3. Layer the carrot slices in bottom of 8 lightly oiled 6-ounce custard cups. Spoon chicken mixture over carrots, smoothing top of mixture. Cover cups tightly with aluminum foil; place in a baking pan. Pour boiling water into baking pan, halfway up sides of custard cups.
4. Bake at 325°F 40 to 45 minutes, or until mixture is set. Remove cups from water. Remove foil. Let stand 5 minutes.
5. Terrines can be served hot, or refrigerated until chilled and served cold. To unmold, run knife around edge of cups and invert on individual plates. Garnish with watercress. Serve with Cucumber Sauce, if desired.

Note: For a luncheon entrée, follow directions above, using six 10-ounce glass dishes. Bake until mixture is set.

Individual Chicken Terrines

Cucumber Sauce

ABOUT
2 CUPS

1 medium cucumber, pared,
seeded, and finely chopped
Chicken Stock (below)
1½ cups Low-Fat Yogurt
(below)
1 tablespoon snipped fresh
or 1½ teaspoons dried dill
weed
¼ teaspoon salt
Dash freshly ground white
pepper

1. Simmer cucumber in 1 inch of stock in a covered saucepan until tender (about 5 minutes); drain off and discard stock.
2. Mix cucumbers with remaining ingredients. Serve cold, or heat and serve warm.

Note: Snipped coriander or mint can be used in place of dill in this recipe.

Chicken Stock

3 TO 3½
QUARTS

5 pounds chicken backs and
wings, or stewing chicken,
cut up
3 carrots, cut in 2-inch
pieces
2 medium yellow onions,
quartered
1 stalk celery, cut in 2-inch
pieces
2 teaspoons salt
Bouquet garni:
    ¾ teaspoon dried thyme
    leaves
    ¾ teaspoon dried rosemary
    leaves
    1 bay leaf
    4 sprigs parsley
    2 whole cloves
Water

1. Place chicken, vegetables, salt, and bouquet garni in an 8-quart Dutch oven. Pour in water to cover (about 4 quarts). Simmer covered 2 to 2½ hours.
2. Strain stock through a double thickness of cheesecloth into a storage container. Taste for seasoning. If more concentrated flavor is desired, return stock to saucepan and simmer 20 to 30 minutes, or dissolve 1 to 2 teaspoons instant chicken bouillon in the stock.
3. Store covered in refrigerator or freezer. Remove solidified fat from top of stock before using.

Note: Refrigerated stock is perishable. If not used within several days, heat to boiling, cool, and refrigerate or freeze to prevent spoilage. Stock can be kept frozen up to 4 months.

Low-Fat Yogurt

ABOUT
1 QUART

1 quart 2% milk
¼ cup instant nonfat
dry-milk
2 tablespoons low-fat natural
yogurt

1. Mix milk and dry-milk solids in a medium saucepan. Heat to scalding (150°F); cool to 110°F. Stir in yogurt.
2. Transfer mixture to a glass or crockery bowl. Cover with plastic wrap; wrap bowl securely in a heavy bath towel. Set in warm place (100° to 125°F)* for 4 to 6 hours, until yogurt has formed.
3. Place several layers of paper toweling directly on yogurt; refrigerate covered until cold.

*A gas oven with a pilot light will be about 125°F; however, use an oven thermometer, as temperature is very important. Turn an electric oven to as warm a setting as necessary to maintain temperature.

Excess liquid and a coarse texture will result if temperature is too high. Liquid can be drained with a nylon baster. Blend yogurt in a food processor or blender to restore texture.

Note: This recipe can be made using skim or reconstituted dry milk, although the product will not be as rich.

Purchased low-fat natural yogurt can be substituted in any recipe.

Pâté à La Maison Grand Vefour

SERVES 6

Dough
2 cups flour
1 egg
3 ounces water
7 ounces butter
salt

Filling
1 pound ground veal
1 pound ground pork
2 egg yolks
salt
pepper
chervil
tarragon
chopped parsley
½ pound cooked ham
Chopped truffles

1. Combine all ingredients for the dough and roll out to ⅓-inch thick.
2. For the filling make a mixture of the ground meat by grinding veal, and pork together, add egg yolks, and season with salt and pepper and the other spices.
3. Add the cooked ham and the truffles, and place the mixture on the dough.
4. Roll the dough around the mixture (save a little for decoration) and pinch it together at both ends. Place it on a baking sheet. Cut a small strip of the dough and make a band. Place it on top of the roll where the dough sides are overlapping. Seal the band with a beaten egg. This band will keep the dough sealed.
5. Put two "chimneys" of waxed paper in the roll. This will allow all the liquid to evaporate and the paté will be firm.
6. Bake in a medium hot oven (350°- 400°F) for about 1½ hours, for a paté of 4 pounds.
7. Remove the "chimneys." Cover the holes with small decorative lids made from leftover dough and brown.

Liver Pâté

10 TO 12 SERVINGS

1½ cups chopped onion
1 cup chopped celery
1½ cups chicken stock
1 cup dry white wine
1 teaspoon paprika
⅛ teaspoon ground allspice or cloves
¼ teaspoon garlic powder
4 drops Tabasco
1¼ teaspoons salt
1½ pounds chicken livers, membranes removed
2 envelopes unflavored gelatin
½ cup cold water
Assorted vegetable relishes

1. Simmer onion and celery in stock and wine in an uncovered saucepan until liquid is reduced to 2 cups (about 15 minutes). Stir in paprika, allspice, garlic powder, Tabasco, and salt; simmer 2 minutes. Stir in livers; simmer covered until livers are tender (about 15 minutes). Drain; discard liquid.
2. Sprinkle gelatin over cold water; let stand 3 minutes. Set over low heat, stirring occasionally, until gelatin is dissolved (about 5 minutes).
3. Purée half the livers and vegetables along with half the gelatin mixture in a food processor or blender. Repeat with remaining ingredients, combine the two mixtures.
4. Pour mixture into a lightly oiled 1½-quart mold or bowl or ten 6-ounce custard cups. Chill until set (about 4 hours).
5. Serve from mold, or unmold onto platter and accompany with assorted vegetables.

Pork Pâté

ABOUT 4 POUNDS

1½ pounds ground fresh pork
½ pound salt pork, diced
5 medium onions, quartered
2 pounds sliced pork liver
3 eggs, beaten
1½ teaspoons salt
½ teaspoon black pepper
1 teaspoon marjoram
½ teaspoon allspice
1 tablespoon beef flavor base
½ pound sliced bacon

1. Combine fresh pork and salt pork in a roasting pan. Roast at 325°F 1 hour, stirring occasionally.
2. Remove pork from pan and set aside. Put onions and liver into the pan. Roast 20 minutes, or until liver is tender. Discard liquid in pan or use for soup.
3. Combine pork, liver, and onion. Grind twice.
4. Add eggs, dry seasonings, and beef flavor base to ground mixture; mix well.
5. Line a 9 x 5 x 3-inch loaf pan (crosswise) with bacon slices. Pack ground mixture into pan. Place remaining bacon (lengthwise) over top of ground mixture.
6. Bake at 325°F 1 hour. Cool in pan.
7. Remove pâté from pan. Chill.
8. To serve, slice pâté and serve cold with **dill pickles** and **horseradish**.

Pâté à La Maison Grand Vefour

Fish and Shellfish Appetizers

Russian Salmon Mound

12 SERVINGS

Pastry:
4 cups flour
2 sticks butter, frozen and cut in 12 pieces
6 tablespoons shortening
1 teaspoon salt
12 tablespoons ice water

Salmon:
3 quarts water
2 cups dry white wine
1 large onion, peeled and quartered
2 stalks celery, trimmed and cut in 1-inch pieces
2 carrots, pared and cut in 1-inch pieces
10 peppercorns
1 tablespoon salt
2½ pounds fresh salmon

Mushroom-Rice Filling:
8 tablespoons butter (1 stick)
½ cup uncooked rice
1¼ cups chicken stock
1 tablespoon dried dill
½ pound fresh mushrooms, cleaned and trimmed
3 tablespoons lemon juice
3 large onions, peeled and quartered
1½ teaspoons salt
¼ teaspoon pepper
3 hard-cooked eggs

Cream Sauce:
2 tablespoons buter
3½ tablespoons flour
2 cups milk, heated
¼ teaspoon salt
Dash pepper

Assembly:
2 tablespoons soft butter
1 egg yolk
1 tablespoon cream
1 tablespoon melted butter

1. To make pastry, using **steel blade** of food processor, place 2 cups flour, 1 stick butter cut in 6 pieces, 3 tablespoons vegetable shortening, and ½ teaspoon salt in a bowl. Process until butter and shortening are cut into flour. With machine on, add 6 tablespoons ice water through feed tube. Process until dough forms into a ball and remove from bowl.
2. Repeat procedure again, using same amounts of ingredients. Wrap both balls of dough in plastic wrap and place in refrigerator to chill while preparing remainder of recipe.
3. To cook salmon, combine 3 quarts water and wine in a large pot.
4. Using **steel blade,** chop onion, celery, and carrots together. Add to pot. Also add peppercorns and salt. Bring to boiling over high heat. Add salmon to liquid, reduce heat, and simmer for about 10 minutes until tender. Remove from pot and separate into small flakes with a fork. Also remove any bones and skin from fish. Set aside.
5. To make filling, melt 2 tablespoons butter in a saucepan, add rice and cook 2 to 3 minutes until rice is coated with butter. Add chicken stock, bring to a boil, and cover. Reduce heat and cook about 20 minutes until tender and fluffy. Remove from heat and stir in dill with a fork. Set aside.
6. Slice mushrooms with **slicing disc.** Melt 2 tablespoons butter in a skillet, add mushrooms, and cook for 5 minutes. Transfer to a small bowl and toss with lemon juice; set aside.
7. Using **steel blade,** process onions until chopped. Melt 4 tablespoons butter in skillet, add chopped onion, and cook until soft, but not brown. Add mushrooms, salt, and pepper; set aside.
8. Using **plastic blade,** process hard-cooked eggs until finely chopped and set aside.
9. To make Cream Sauce, melt 2 tablespoons butter and add flour. Cook for a minute or two, remove from heat and add heated milk, stirring constantly with a whisk until smooth. Bring to boiling, add salt and pepper, and remove from heat.
10. In a large bowl, combine flaked salmon, mushroom-onion mixture, rice, chopped hard-cooked eggs, and Cream Sauce. Gently toss with two wooden spoons until thoroughly mixed. Adjust seasonings, adding more salt, pepper, and dill as desired.
11. To assemble, roll 1 ball of dough into a rectangle and trim to 15x8 inches. Coat a large cookie sheet with 2 tablespoons butter. Drape pastry around rolling pin and unroll

(continued)

Russian Salmon Mound

over cookie sheet. Place filling in center, forming it into a mound and leaving a 2-inch border around edges. Using a pastry brush, coat border with a mixture of 1 egg yolk and 1 tablespoon cream.

12. Roll other ball of dough into a rectangle 18x11 inches. Roll it around rolling pin and place over salmon mound. Trim borders of dough so that they are even. Turn up border of dough to make a shallow rim around mound and decorate (crimp) at ½-inch intervals with dull side of a knife. Cut a 1-inch circle in center of mound and decorate top with leftover pastry. Brush entire loaf with egg yolk mixture. Pour 1 tablespoon melted butter in opening.

13. Bake at 400°F 1 hour, or until golden. Serve with a pitcher of **melted butter** or bowl of **sour cream.**

Fish Balls

ABOUT 5 DOZ.
FISH BALLS

2 tablespoons butter
¼ cup sifted all-purpose
   flour
1 teaspoon salt
⅛ teaspoon pepper
1 cup cream
3 cups flaked cooked fish
   (cod, trout, fillet of
   sole, whitefish)
1 egg yolk, beaten
2 eggs, slightly beaten
1 cup fine, dry bread
   crumbs

1. Set out a deep saucepan or automatic deep-fryer and heat fat to 350°F.
2. Heat butter over low heat in a saucepan.
3. Blend in flour, salt and pepper.
4. Heat until mixture bubbles. Add cream gradually, stirring constantly.
5. Cook rapidly, stirring constantly, until mixture thickens. Remove from heat; cool.
6. Meanwhile, flake finely enough cooked fish to yield 3 cups.
7. When sauce is cool, blend in the fish and 1 egg yolk.
8. Shape mixture into balls 1 in. in diameter. Dip balls into 2 eggs.
9. To coat evenly, roll balls in bread crumbs.
10. Deep-fry Fish Balls in heated fat. Deep-fry only as many balls at one time as will float uncrowded one-layer deep in the fat. Turn balls often. Deep-fry 2 min., or until lightly browned. Drain; remove to absorbent paper.
11. Keep Fish Balls warm for the smorgasbord.

Gefilte Fish

ABOUT
20 BALLS

3 pounds fresh fish
   (whitefish, carp, and/or
   pike)
2 quarts water
2 teaspoons salt
½ teaspoon pepper
8 carrots, pared
4 medium onions, peeled and
   cut to fit feed tube
2 eggs
6 tablespoons ice water
4 tablespoons matzoh meal
2 teaspoons salt
½ teaspoon pepper

1. Have fish filleted, reserving head, bones, and skin.
2. In a large pot, place water, 2 teaspoons salt, ½ teaspoon pepper, 7 carrots, head, bones, and skin of fish.
3. Using **slicing disc** of food processor, slice 3½ onions (cut remaining ½ onion in half and reserve). Add sliced onion to the pot, bring to a boil, lower heat, and simmer while fish is being prepared.
4. Cut fish into 2-inch pieces. Using **steel blade**, process fish in 1-pound batches to pastelike consistency. Remove to a large bowl and repeat 2 more times with remaining fish. After all fish has been processed, thoroughly mix together by hand to blend fish together.
5. Using **steel blade**, process remaining carrot and ½ onion together until finely chopped. Remove half of this mixture from the bowl.

6. Add half of fish mixture to the bowl. To this add 1 egg, 3 tablespoons ice water, 2 tablespoons matzoh meal, 1 teaspoon salt, and ¼ teaspoon pepper. Process, using quick on/off motions, until thoroughly blended. Remove mixture from bowl and repeat procedure, using remaining ingredients.

7. Remove head bones, and skin of fish from stock.

8. With wet hands, shape fish into shapes the size of a small baking potato and place in fish stock. Simmer slowly 2 hours.

9. Remove fish balls with a slotted spoon and place on a lettuce-lined platter. Cool and chill. Cool fish stock and save for later use for storing leftover fish.

10. Garnish with pieces of cooked carrots left over from stock and serve with freshly made horseradish.

Horseradish

½ cup horseradish root, cut in 1-inch cubes
Beet juice

Using **steel blade** of food processor, process until finely chopped. Add a few drops of beet juice to get desired color. Step back from bowl before removing lid.

Broiled Fish Quenelles

8 SERVINGS

2 pounds skinned fish fillets
  (all trout or a combination
  of trout, whitefish, or pike)
½ cup chopped onion
⅓ cup chopped carrot
1 egg, beaten
2 teaspoons vegetable oil
1½ teaspoons salt
1½ teaspoons matzo meal or
  white cornmeal
3 tablespoons ice water
Watercress

1. Place all ingredients except 1 tablespoon of the ice water and watercress in a blender or food processor; purée until the consistency of a paste. Add remaining ice water if necessary (mixture should hold together and be easy to handle).
2. Form fish mixture into oval patties, using ½ cup for each. Place on a lightly oiled cookie sheet.
3. Broil 4 inches from heat until patties are well browned and slightly puffed (8 to 10 minutes on each side). Serve immediately. Garnish with watercress.

Pickled Herring

10 TO 12 SERVINGS

3 qts. cold water
2 salt herring, cleaned and
  cut into fillets
1 large onion
1 cup cider vinegar
1 cup water
1 tablespoon peppercorns
1 bay leaf

1. Pour 3 qts. cold water into a large bowl.
2. Put herring into the water. Set aside to soak 3 hrs. (To prepare Herring, see below.)
3. Clean onion and thinly slice.
4. Separate onion slices into rings.
5. Mix cider vinegar, water, peppercorns, and bay leaf together.
6. Drain herring and cut into 2-in. square pieces. Put a layer of herring into a shallow bowl and top with some of the onion rings. Repeat layers of herring and onion. Pour over the vinegar-water mixture. Chill thoroughly in refrigerator several hours or overnight to blend flavors.
7. When ready to serve, drain off liquid. Toss herring and onion lightly to mix and put into a serving bowl. Garnish with sprigs of parsley.

To Prepare Herring—With a sharp knife cut off and discard head. Slit along underside of the fish from head to tail. Remove entrails and scrape insides well. Cut off tail and fins. Rinse thoroughly in cold water. Cut off a strip about ½ in. wide along each of cut edges. Discard strips. Make a slip along backbone just to the bone. Using a sharp knife, carefully pull and scrape the blue skin from the flesh. Be careful not to tear fish. Then cut along backbone through bone and flesh to remove one side of fish. Repeat for the second side. Remove as many of the small bones as possible without tearing fish.

Anchovy Fillets

½ pound anchovy fillets
  preserved in salt
Wine vinegar (2 or more
  cups)
2 tablespoons olive oil

1. Separate fillets. Scrape scales and as much of the salt as possible from each fillet.
2. Soak in wine vinegar 5 to 10 minutes, changing as often as necessary until the vinegar remains clear.
3. Drain fillets on paper towels.
4. Arrange fillets on a serving platter. Drizzle with 1 tablespoon fresh vinegar and the olive oil.
5. Serve as an hors d'oeuvre or in anchovy salad.

Eggs with Anchovies

8 EGG HALVES

4 hard-cooked eggs
Lettuce leaves
16 anchovy fillets
2 tablespoons mayonnaise
1 dill pickle, sliced
1 tomato, sliced

1. Peel the eggs; cut in halves.
2. Arrange eggs, yolks up, on a dish covered with lettuce leaves.
3. Place 2 anchovy fillets over each egg to form an "X."
4. Garnish with mayonnaise, pickle, and tomato slices.

Seviche

8 SERVINGS
(½ CUP EACH)

1¼ pounds whitefish fillets, skinned and cut in 2 x ¼-inch strips
1 cup fresh lemon juice
2 green chiles, seeded and minced
1 teaspoon snipped fresh or ½ teaspoon dried oregano leaves
1 tablespoon snipped fresh or 1½ teaspoons dried coriander leaves
1 tablespoon olive oil
1 teaspoon salt
¼ teaspoon freshly ground pepper
2 large tomatoes, peeled, seeded, and chopped
1 medium green pepper, finely chopped
1 small yellow onion, finely chopped
¼ cup fresh lime juice
Radish slices
Ripe olives

1. Place fish in a shallow glass bowl; pour lemon juice over it. Refrigerate covered 6 hours, stirring occasionally. Drain; discard lemon juice.
2. Mix remaining ingredients except radish slices and olives with fish in a medium bowl. Refrigerate 30 minutes.
3. Serve on chilled plates; garnish with radish slices and olives. Or spoon into **fluted lemon shells.**

Crab Meat and Bean Sprouts with Omelet Strips

4 SERVINGS

2 eggs
3 tablespoons water
1 tablespoon dry sherry
1 tablespoon light soy sauce
1 tablespoon walnut or vegetable oil
4 green onions, chopped
¾ cup chopped green pepper
1 cup sliced fresh mushrooms
2 cups drained fresh or canned bean sprouts
8 ounces fresh or 1 can (7 ¾ ounces) crab meat, drained and flaked
1 teaspoon toasted sesame seed

1. Beat eggs with water, sherry, and 1 tablespoon soy sauce. Heat half the walnut oil in a small skillet. Cook egg mixture in skillet until set but still moist on top; remove to plate and cut egg into strips.
2. Heat remaining walnut oil in a wok or medium skillet. Cook and stir vegetables and 1 tablespoon soy sauce until vegetables are just tender (about 3 minutes). Add crab meat and omelet strips; cook and stir until thoroughly heated (about 1 minute). Sprinkle with toasted sesame seed. Serve immediately.

Crab Meat Newburg Appetizer

25 SERVINGS

2 tablespoons butter or
  margarine
2 tablespoons flour
½ teaspoon salt
2 cups milk
2 cups (8 ounces) shredded
  Cheddar cheese
2 cans (7½ ounces each)
  Alaska King crab, drained
  and flaked
3 hard-cooked eggs, grated
½ cup finely chopped onion
Dash ground red pepper
1 tablespoon snipped parsley

1. Melt butter in a saucepan. Add flour and salt. Gradually add milk, stirring until thickened and smooth.
2. Add cheese, stirring until blended. Blend in remaining ingredients, except parsley. Put into a 1½-quart casserole.
3. Bake, covered, at 325°F 15 minutes, or until heated through. Sprinkle with parsley. Serve with **Melba toast** or **toast-points.**

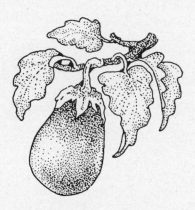

Avocado Voisin

6 SERVINGS

4 tablespoons butter
1½ tablespoons minced onion
1½ tablespoons minced
  celery
¾ teaspoon curry powder
¾ cup uncooked white rice
1½ cups chicken or beef
  broth
Salt
White pepper
1 small bay leaf
2 tablespoons flour
1 cup milk
1 egg yolk
2 cans (about 6½ ounces
  each), crab meat, drained
2 tablespoons chutney, finely
  chopped
3 large avocados
Lemon juice
3 tablespoons grated
  Parmesan cheese
Parsley and lemon wedges
  for garnish

1. Melt 1½ tablespoons butter in skillet. Add onion and celery; cook until tender, about 4 minutes, stirring occasionally.
2. Add curry powder to vegetables and blend thoroughly. Stir in rice, mixing to coat each grain. Add broth, few grains each salt and white pepper, and bay leaf. Bring to boiling, cover, lower heat, and simmer until moisture is absorbed and rice is tender (about 20 minutes).
3. In a saucepan, melt 1½ tablespoons butter. Blend in flour and a few grains each salt and white pepper. Cook slowly for 5 minutes, not allowing mixture to brown. Remove pan from heat and stir milk gradually into flour mixture. Return pan to heat, cook until sauce is thickened (about 10 minutes), stirring constantly.
4. Beat a small amount of hot mixture into egg yolk, then return to mixture in saucepan. Heat just to boiling. Remove from heat, cover, and keep warm.
5. Sauté crab meat in 1 tablespoon butter 1 minute. Add chutney and mix well. Combine cooked rice and crab meat, tossing lightly to mix. Keep warm.
6. Halve avocados, remove seeds, and peel. Cut small slice from bottoms so that avocados will be flat. Put cut-off slices in avocado cavities, and brush cut surfaces of avocado with lemon juice.
7. Arrange avocado halves in a shallow baking dish. Pile crab-rice mixture into avocado halves. Spoon sauce over each stuffed avocado. Sprinkle with Parmesan cheese.
8. Bake at 300°F 10 to 15 minutes.
9. Garnish with parsley and lemon wedges.

Avocado Voisin

Pickled Shrimp

ABOUT
25 APPETIZERS

1 can or bottle (12 ounces) beer
¼ cup oil
1 tablespoon lemon juice
1 teaspoon sugar
1 teaspoon salt
½ teaspoon each dill seed, dry mustard, and celery salt
¼ teaspoon tarragon
⅛ teaspoon ground red pepper
2 bay leaves, halved
2 medium onion, chopped
1 package (10 ounces) small to medium frozen cooked shrimp, thawed

1. Place all ingredients except shrimp in a saucepan. Simmer 10 to 15 minutes, or until onions are just tender.
2. Add shrimp; remove from heat. Turn into a small casserole. Cover and refrigerate at least 1 day.
3. Remove bay leaves; drain off marinade. Let guests spoon shrimp and onions onto **cocktail rye rounds.**

Note: With larger shrimp to be served on fancy picks, use only one onion and slice it. Remove onion before serving. Recipe may also be made with uncooked shrimp. Add them 4 to 5 minutes before end of cooking time; cover and simmer until shrimp turn pink. Continue as in above recipe.

Shrimp Dunk

25 TO 30
SHRIMP

1 can or bottle (12 ounces) beer plus ½ cup water
1 small onion, sliced
Top and leaves of 1 stalk celery
1 tablespoon salt
3 or 4 peppercorns
1 bay leaf
1 garlic clove
1 pound very large shelled shrimp, uncooked

1. Combine ingredients except shrimp in a large saucepan. Cover; heat to boiling. Boil 10 minutes.
2. Add shrimp. Cover and boil 5 minutes, or just until shrimp turn pink. Remove from heat; chill in cooking liquid.
3. Serve cold with dunking bowls of cold beer. Serve as hors d'oeuvres or as a summertime main entrée.

Shrimp Cocktail

ABOUT
3 CUPS SHRIMP

1½ lbs. fresh shrimp with shells
3 cups water
3 tablespoons lemon juice
1 tablespoon salt
1 bay leaf

1. Wash shrimp in cold water.
2. Drop shrimp into a boiling mixture of water, lemon juice, salt and bay leaf.
3. Cover tightly. Simmer 5 min., or until shrimp are pink and tender. Drain shrimp and cover with cold water to chill. Drain shrimp again. Remove tiny legs. Peel shells from the shrimp. Cut a slit along back (outer curved surface) of shrimp to expose the black vein. With knife point, remove vein in one piece. Rinse the shrimp quickly in cold

water. Drain them on absorbent paper. Store in refrigerator until ready to use.

4. Serve shrimp on **lettuce** or **curly endive.** Top with **Peppy Cocktail Sauce.**

Note: Veins present in canned or frozen shrimp are removed in the same way.

Hot Shrimp Appetizer: Follow recipe for Shrimp Cocktail. Arrange shrimp on broiler rack. Brush with a mixture of ½ cup **butter** or *margarine,* melted, and 3 tablespoons **lemon juice.** Set temperature control of range at Broil. Place broiler rack about 2 in. from source of heat for 3 to 5 min., or until shrimp are thoroughly heated. Insert wooden picks. Serve immediately with **Peppy Cocktail Sauce.**

Oysters Rockefeller

4 TO 6
SERVINGS

2 tablespoons butter or
  margarine
2 tablespoons flour
½ teaspoon salt
⅛ teaspoon pepper
1 cup milk (use light cream
  for richer sauce)
1 egg, well beaten
2 dozen oysters in shells
2 tablespoons sherry
2 tablespoons butter or
  margarine
1 tablespoon finely chopped
  onion
1 pound fresh spinach,
  cooked, drained, and finely
  chopped
1 tablespoon minced parsley
½ teaspoon Worcestershire
  sauce
6 drops Tabasco
¼ teaspoon salt
Few grains ground nutmeg
¼ cup shredded Parmesan
  cheese

1. For sauce, heat 2 tablespoons butter in a saucepan. Blend in flour, salt, and pepper; heat and stir until bubbly.
2. Gradually add the milk, stirring until smooth. Bring to boiling; cook and stir 1 to 2 minutes longer.
3. Stir the egg into white sauce; set aside.
4. Pour **coarse salt** into a 15 x 10 x 1-inch jelly roll pan to a ¼-inch depth. Open oysters and arrange the oysters, in the shells, on the salt; sprinkle ¼ teaspoon sherry over each.
5. Heat 2 tablespoons butter in a heavy skillet. Add the onion and cook until partially tender. Add the chopped spinach, 2 tablespoons of the white sauce, parsley, Worcestershire sauce, and Tabasco to the skillet along with salt and nutmeg; mix thoroughly. Heat 2 to 3 minutes.
6. Spoon spinach mixture over all of the oysters; spoon remaining white sauce over spinach. Sprinkle each oyster with cheese.
7. Bake at 375°F 15 to 20 minutes, or until tops are lightly browned.

Pickled Octopus

4 TO 6
SERVINGS

1 small octopus (about 2
  pounds)
½ cup olive oil
¼ cup white wine vinegar
Juice of ½ lemon
1 tablespoon minced parsley
½ teaspoon marjoram
Salt and pepper to taste

1. Beat octopus with the flat side of a metal meat hammer 15 to 20 minutes; it will feel soft and excrete a grayish liquid.
2. Wash octopus thoroughly, drain, and cook in skillet without water until it becomes bright pink. Cut into bite-size pieces.
3. Make a salad dressing of the olive oil, vinegar, lemon juice, parsley, marjoram, salt, and pepper. Mix well.
4. Pour over octopus and store in the refrigerator in a covered container for 5 days before serving.
5. Serve cold as an appetizer.

Poultry and Meat Appetizers

Ham and Egg Rolls

12 ROLLS

6 hard-cooked eggs
12 thin slices cooked ham
Lettuce leaves
Mayonnaise
Pickles

1. Peel the eggs; cut in halves.
2. Roll each half of egg in a slice of ham. Secure with wooden pick.
3. Arrange lettuce leaves around ham and egg rolls on serving plate. Decorate with mayonnaise and garnish with pickles.

Cheddar-Sausage Rolls

ABOUT 1½ DOZEN APPETIZERS

1 cup (4 ounces) shredded Cheddar cheese, at room temperature
3 tablespoons sour cream
6 slices summer sausage, about 4½ inches in diameter

1. Combine cheese and sour cream in a small bowl.
2. Remove casings from sausage. Spread a scant 2 tablespoons cheese mixture on each slice of sausage. Place one slice of sausage on top of another, overlapping one half of the way. Roll sausage firmly and wrap. Repeat twice to form 3 rolls. Chill.
3. To serve, cut into ½-inch slices.

Chicken Tantalizers in Cherry Sauce

50 APPETIZERS

2 pounds chicken breasts and thighs, skinned, boned, and cut into 1-inch pieces
1 egg, beaten
6 tablespoons cornstarch
3 tablespoons cooking oil
1 can (8 ounces) pitted dark sweet cherries (undrained)
2 tablespoons sugar
1½ teaspoons cornstarch
1 tablespoon soy sauce
¼ cup vinegar

1. Dip chicken pieces in beaten egg, and coat with 6 tablespoons cornstarch.
2. Heat oil in a skillet and quickly brown chicken.
3. Purée undrained cherries in an electric blender, pour into cooking pan of chafing dish, and heat gently over low heat. Combine sugar, 1½ teaspoons cornstarch, soy sauce, and vinegar. Add gradually to cherry mixture while stirring. Bring to boiling over medium heat and boil 1 minute, or until sauce is thickened and clear.
4. Add chicken to sauce, mixing gently. Heat thoroughly.
5. Keep warm while serving. Accompany with picks.

Oriental Chicken Wings

10 chicken wings
½ cup soy sauce
2 tablespoons sugar
1 tablespoon dry sherry
½ teaspoon anise seed
⅓ cup water

1. Cut tips off chicken wings and discard. Cut wings in two at joints. Wash in warm water and dry.
2. In a heavy saucepan, combine chicken wings and remaining ingredients. Bring to boiling, reduce heat, cover, and simmer 20 minutes; stir occasionally.

3. Remove cover and simmer another 15 minutes, basting frequently until about ½ cup liquid remains.
4. Turn into cooking pan of a chafing dish, spoon liquid over wings, and serve while hot.

20 APPETIZERS

Note: If desired, the prepared chicken wings may be refrigerated in the sauce overnight for a stronger flavor and reheated in chafing dish before serving.

Teriyaki

ABOUT
24 APPETIZERS

1 teaspoon ground ginger
⅓ cup soy sauce
¼ cup honey
1 clove garlic, minced
1 teaspoon grated onion
1 pound beef sirloin tip, cut into 2x½x¼-inch strips
2 to 3 tablespoons cooking oil
1 tablespoon cornstarch
½ cup water
⅛ teaspoon red food coloring

1. Blend ginger; soy sauce, honey, garlic, and onion in a bowl. Add meat; marinate about 1 hour.
2. Remove meat, reserving marinade, and brown quickly on all sides in the hot oil in a large wok. Remove meat from wok.
3. Stir a blend of cornstarch, water, and food coloring into the reserved marinade and pour into wok. Bring rapidly to boiling and cook 2 to 3 minutes, stirring constantly.
4. Add meat to thickened marinade to glaze; remove and drain on wire rack.
5. Insert a frilled wooden pick into each meat strip and serve with the thickened marinade.

Steak Tartare with Vegetables

8 SERVINGS

2 pounds beef sirloin steak, boneless
⅓ cup finely chopped leek or green onion
1½ teaspoons Worcestershire sauce
¼ teaspoon Tabasco
1 teaspoon Dijon mustard
½ teaspoon salt
Freshly ground Szechuan or black pepper
1 egg yolk, if desired
1 teaspoon drained capers
2 bunches parsley, stems removed
1 green pepper, cut in 1-inch pieces
1 sweet red pepper, cut in 1-inch pieces
1 large zucchini, cut in ¼-inch slices
1 medium cucumber, cut in ¼-inch slices
12 medium mushrooms, cut in half lengthwise
1 large carrot, cut in ¼-inch slices
12 large red or white radishes, cut in half

1. Chop meat coarsely in a food processor (or have butcher grind meat coarsely 2 times). Place beef, leek, Worcestershire sauce, Tabasco, mustard, salt, and pepper in a mixing bowl; mix quickly and lightly with 2 forks. Taste; adjust seasonings.
2. Mound beef on a medium serving platter. Make an indentation in top of mound; slip egg yolk into indentation. Sprinkle beef with capers. Surround beef with a thick rim of parsley. Arrange vegetables on parsley. Serve immediately with knives for spreading beef mixture on vegetables.

Note: For a party, this recipe would make about 48 appetizer servings.

Spicy Steak Tartare

1 small green onion, cleaned, trimmed, and cut in 1-inch pieces
2 tablespoons fresh parsley, cleaned and trimmed (1 tablespoon chopped)
1 radish, cleaned and trimmed
½ pound beef (sirloin, tenderloin, or fillet), cut in 1-inch cubes
1 egg yolk
1 tablespoon lemon juice
1 tablespoon capers
Drop of Dijon mustard
Salt
Freshly ground black pepper to taste
3 drops Tabasco

Using **steel blade** of food processor, process green onion, parsley, and radish together until finely chopped. Add meat and remaining ingredients and process, using quick on/off motions, to desired consistency. Serve with triangles of **black bread.**

Swedish Meat Balls

ABOUT
3 DOZEN
MEAT BALLS

1 cup (3 slices) fine, dry bread crumbs
1 lb. ground round steak
½ lb. ground pork
½ cup mashed potatoes
1 egg, beaten
1 teaspoon salt
½ teaspoon brown sugar
¼ teaspoon pepper
¼ teaspoon allspice
¼ teaspoon nutmeg
⅛ teaspoon cloves
⅛ teaspoon ginger
3 tablespoons butter

1. Set out a large, heavy skillet having a tight-fitting cover.
2. Set out bread crumbs.
3. Lightly mix together in a large bowl ½ cup of the bread crumbs and steak, pork, potatoes, egg and a mixture of salt, brown sugar, pepper, allspice, nutmeg, cloves, and ginger.
4. Shape mixture into balls about 1 in. in diameter. Roll balls lightly in remaining crumbs.
5. Heat the butter in the skillet over low heat.
6. Add the meat balls and brown on all sides. Shake pan frequently to brown evenly and to keep balls round. Cover and cook about 15 minutes, or until meat balls are thoroughly cooked.

Veal Picks

ABOUT 1 DOZ.
APPETIZERS

½ cup ground cooked veal
¼ cup pecans (about ¼ cup, ground)
1 pkg. (3 oz.) cream cheese, softened
2 tablespoons (about ½ oz.) crumbled Blue cheese
1½ teaspoons Worcestershire sauce
Few grains paprika

1. Grind cooked veal and set aside.
2. Grind pecans and set aside.
3. Cream together cream cheese, softened and crumbled Blue cheese.
4. Combine with cheese and veal and mix Worcestershire sauce and paprika thoroughly.
5. Shape into balls about ¾ in. in diameter. Coat with ground pecans. Insert cocktail or wooden picks and place in refrigerator to chill.

Veal-Parsley Picks: Follow recipe for Veal Picks. Omit Blue cheese. Substitute ¼ cup minced **parsley** for pecans. Roll balls in parsley before inserting picks.

Lamb Kabobs

6 SERVINGS

1½ pounds lamb (leg, loin, or shoulder), boneless, cut in 1½-inch cubes
½ cup vegetable oil
1 tablespoon lemon juice
2 teaspoons sugar
½ teaspoon salt
½ teaspoon paprika
¼ teaspoon dry mustard
⅛ teaspoon ground black pepper
¼ teaspoon Worcestershire sauce
1 clove garlic, cut in halves
6 small whole cooked potatoes
6 small whole cooked onions
Butter or margarine, melted
6 plum tomatoes

1. Put lamb cubes into a shallow dish. Combine oil, lemon juice, sugar, salt, paprika, dry mustard, pepper, Worcestershire sauce, and garlic. Pour over meat. Cover and marinate at least 1 hour in refrigerator, turning pieces occasionally. Drain.
2. Alternately thread lamb cubes, potatoes, and onions on 6 skewers. Brush pieces with melted butter.
3. Broil 3 to 4 inches from heat about 15 minutes, or until lamb is desired degree of doneness; turn frequently and brush with melted butter. Shortly before kabobs are done, impale tomatoes on ends of skewers.

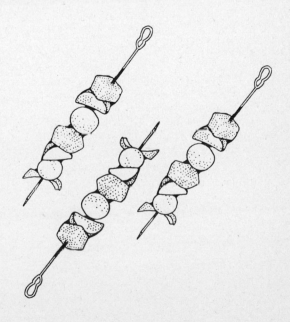

Vegetable Appetizers

Chilled Artichoke Plate

4 SERVINGS

4 medium artichokes
Chicken Stock (page 43)
¼ cup lemon juice
1 teaspoon salt
½ pint cherry tomatoes
¾ cup Mock Béarnaise
  Sauce (below)
1 pound fresh asparagus, cut
  in 2-inch pieces

1. Snip tips from artichoke leaves with scissors. Simmer artichokes in 1 inch of the stock with lemon juice and salt in a large covered saucepan until tender (about 45 minutes). Lift from pan with tongs; let cool. Refrigerate until chilled.
2. Carefully scoop seeds from tomatoes, using small end of a melon-ball cutter. Fill tomatoes with ¼ cup of the sauce; refrigerate.
3. Scrape choke from artichoke bottoms. Place artichokes in center of individual plates and dollop each with 2 tablespoons sauce. Arrange raw asparagus pieces and tomatoes attractively on plates. Serve immediately.

Chilled Artichoke Plate

Mock Hollandaise Sauce

¾ CUP

½ cup Neufchatel cheese
3 tablespoons Low-Fat
  Yogurt (page 43)
Dash salt
Juice of ½ lemon

1. Mix all ingredients in a blender or food processor until smooth and fluffy.
2. Cook over simmering water until hot and thickened. Serve immediately or refrigerate and serve cold. Stir before using.

Mock Béarnaise Sauce: Stir 1½ teaspoons snipped fresh or ½ teaspoon dried tarragon leaves and ½ teaspoon minced shallots into sauce before heating.

Mock Mayonnaise: Stir 1½ teaspoons Dijon mustard and ½ teaspoon sugar into sauce before heating. Refrigerate until cold.

Note: The above sauces can be refrigerated up to 3 weeks.

George's Greek-Style Artichokes

ABOUT
8 SERVINGS

6 artichokes
4 ounces fresh mushrooms, sliced
⅔ cup coarsely chopped onion
½ cup olive oil
½ cup dry white wine
Juice of 1 lemon
30 fennel seeds
¼ teaspoon coriander
Salt and pepper to taste

1. Rinse artichokes and discard the hard outer leaves. Quarter artichokes, remove and discard "choke" or fuzzy part, and arrange the pieces in a large baking pan or shallow heat-resistant casserole having a cover. Allow plenty of space for the artichokes.
2. Cover artichoke pieces with the mushrooms and onion. Then pour over them a mixture of oil, wine, lemon juice, and dry seasonings.
3. Cover and place over medium heat. Bring to a rapid boil and cook about 1 minute.
4. Set in a 350°F oven about 30 minutes, or until artichokes are tender.
5. Remove from oven; cool at room temperature, then refrigerate to chill thoroughly. Serve cold.

Stuffed Grape Leaves

ABOUT
50 STUFFED
GRAPE LEAVES

1 jar (32 ounces) grapevine leaves
1 quart water
½ cup olive oil
3 medium onions, finely chopped
1½ cups long-grain rice
Juice of 2 lemons
2 tablespoons pine nuts
1 tablespoon dried black currants
2 teaspoons dill
2 teaspoons mint
¼ cup minced parsley
Salt and pepper to taste
Water (about 1 cup)
Olive oil (about 1 cup)

1. To prepare grapevine leaves, rinse leaves thoroughly in cold running water to remove brine.
2. Bring 1 quart water to a boil. Add leaves and parboil 3 minutes. Drain.
3. Select 4 or 5 heavy leaves and line bottom of a medium-size Dutch oven. Set aside.
4. To prepare filling, heat ½ cup olive oil in a medium skillet. Add onion and cook until translucent. Remove with a slotted spoon.
5. In a saucepan, parboil rice in 1 cup water until liquid is absorbed.
6. Combine rice, onion, lemon juice, pine nuts, currants, dill, mint, and parsley. Season with salt and pepper. Cool.
7. To fill grapevine leaves, place a leaf on a working surface, rough side up with stem pointing toward you. Place about a teaspoon of the rice mixture at the base of the leaf. Lift the bottom sides of the leaf up onto the filling. Fold both the right and left sides of the leaf over the filling. Roll up, tucking the edges in.
8. Place the stuffed grape leaves side by side in the Dutch oven to cover the bottom. Put a second layer on top of the first one. Continue to do this until all the stuffed leaves have been put in.
9. Add water and olive oil to cover. Place an inverted plate on the grape leaves. Bring to boiling. Cover Dutch oven, lower heat, and simmer 1 hour. Taste a stuffed grape leaf to see if rice is tender. If necessary, continue cooking.
10. Cool in liquid. Remove carefully with a spoon. Chill in refrigerator 24 hours before serving. Serve cold.

Note: Stuffed Grape Leaves will keep 10 days in the refrigerator.

Stuffed Celery Rings

SERVES 8

1 medium bunch celery
Tangy cheese spread
French dressing

1. Cut the top from bunch celery.
2. Wash and dry each stalk.
3. Fill smallest stalks with cheese spread, then fill next smallest stalks and press firmly against first stalks.
4. Continue filling and pressing stalks together until all the celery is formed into a bunch. Tie firmly with string; chill.
5. Slice crosswise into thin slices and serve on lettuce or watercress. Sprinkle with French dressing.

Note: If desired, use Roquefort spread instead of tangy cheese spread.

Dill Pickles

4 PINTS
PICKLES

3 pounds 4-inch cucumbers
2 cloves garlic, crushed
1 cup distilled white vinegar
5 cups water
½ cup salt
3 tablespoons dried dill weed

1. Scrub cucumbers.
2. Place a layer of dill on bottom of a large ceramic bowl or crock. Cover with half the cucumbers. Add another layer of dill, then the remaining cucumbers. Add garlic. Top with a final layer of dill.
3. Mix vinegar, water, and salt. Pour over dill and cucumbers. Add more water, if needed, to cover completely.
4. Cover bowl with a china plate to hold pickles under the brine. Let stand in a cool place 4 days.
5. Seal in sterilized jars.

Pickled Carrots

1 PINT PICKLE

6 to 8 medium carrots, pared and cut in strips
Boiling salted water
2 tablespoons olive oil
1 clove garlic, cut in halves
1 hot green pepper
½ teaspoon salt
Wine vinegar

1. Cook carrots in a small amount of boiling salted water in a covered saucepan until just tender. Drain and cool.
2. Pack carrots in a pint screw-top jar and add oil, garlic, hot pepper, and salt. Cover carrots with wine vinegar.
3. Store, covered, in refrigerator at least 24 hours. Drain and serve cold.

Pickled Watermelon Rind

3 PINTS

3 pounds watermelon rind
Salted water (use 3 tablespoons salt for each quart of water)
2 pounds sugar
3 cups distilled white vinegar
6 pieces stick cinnamon (3 inches each)
2 tablespoons whole allspice
2 tablespoons whole cloves
2 tablespoons whole mustard seed

1. Cut rind into 1-inch cubes; trim off outer green skin and bright pink flesh.
2. Soak overnight in enough salted water to cover. Drain.
3. Heat sugar and vinegar to boiling.
4. Tie spices in cheesecloth bag.
5. Add spice bag and melon rind to vinegar mixture. Cook, uncovered, until melon is transparent, about 45 minutes.
6. Discard spice bag.
7. If desired, add a few drops red or green food coloring to the rind.
8. Pack watermelon rind tightly into hot, sterilized jars. Pour boiling syrup over watermelon to within ⅛ inch from top, making sure vinegar solution covers rind. Seal each jar at once.

Pickled Mushrooms

4 PINTS

4 pounds small mushrooms
4 cups boiling water
1½ tablespoons salt

Marinade:
1¾ cups water
15 peppercorns
2 bay leaves
2½ tablespoons salt
¾ cup sugar
¾ cup vinegar

1. Cut the mushroom stems off even with the caps.
2. Cook over medium heat in boiling water with salt until they sink to the bottom, about 10 to 15 minutes.
3. Remove mushroom caps; place in small sterilized jars.
4. Make marinade. Boil water with peppercorns and bay leaves for 30 minutes. Add salt and sugar. Stir until dissolved. Add the vinegar, bring to boiling.
5. Pour hot marinade over mushroom caps. Close the jars. Keep refrigerated 2 or 3 days before serving.

Mushrooms à la Grecque

8 to 10 PORTIONS

1 pound fresh mushrooms or
 2 cans (6 to 8 ounces each)
 whole mushrooms
⅓ cup olive oil
⅓ cup dry white wine or
 apple juice
¼ cup water
1 tablespoon lemon juice
¾ cup chopped onion
1 large clove garlic, minced
1½ teaspoons salt
1 teaspoon sugar
½ teaspoon coriander seed
 (optional)
¼ teaspoon black pepper
2 cups carrot chunks
½ cup pimento-stuffed olives

1. Rinse, pat dry, and halve fresh mushrooms or drain canned mushrooms; set aside.
2. In a large saucepan combine oil, wine, water, lemon juice, onion, garlic, salt, sugar, coriander, and black pepper. Bring to boiling; add carrots.
3. Cover and simmer for 15 minutes. Add mushrooms and olives. Return to boiling; reduce heat. Cover and simmer for 5 minutes.
4. Chill thoroughly, at least overnight.
5. To serve, thread mushrooms, carrot chunks, and olives on skewers or spoon into a bowl. Serve as hors d'oeuvres.

Mushrooms à la Grecque

Vegetable Mélange with Mustard Sauce

6 SERVINGS

1 large yellow squash or zucchini, pared and minced
3 medium carrots, minced
¼ cup minced onion
¼ cup minced dill pickle
4 ounces Swiss cheese,
minced
⅓ cup prepared mustard
⅓ cup dill pickle juice
1 teaspoon sugar
½ teaspoon curry powder
1 garlic clove, minced
Lettuce cups

Combine squash, carrot, onion, pickle, and cheese in a medium bowl. Mix remaining ingredients, except lettuce cups; pour over vegetables and stir to coat well. Refrigerate until well chilled. Serve in lettuce cups.

Flybanes

8 FLYBANES

8 hard-cooked eggs
4 small tomatoes
Salt and pepper
Mayonnaise
Lettuce

1. Peel the eggs. Cut off both ends so eggs will stand evenly. Stand the eggs on a small tray; they will serve for mushroom stems.
2. Cut the tomatoes in halves lengthwise. Remove cores. Sprinkle with salt and pepper. Put each tomato half over an egg as a mushroom cap. Dot the caps with mayonnaise. Garnish the tray with lettuce.

Herbed Stuffed Mushrooms

4 SERVINGS

¾ pound mushrooms,
chopped
¼ teaspoon salt
⅛ teaspoon freshly ground
pepper
1½ teaspoons snipped fresh
or ½ teaspoon dried basil
leaves
1 tablespoon snipped parsley
½ cup chopped onion
8 large mushrooms, stems
removed and sliced into
rounds; reserve caps
2 tablespoons brandy
1 tablespoon clarified butter
Parsley for garnish (optional)

1. Process ¾ pound mushrooms, the salt, pepper, basil, parsley, and onions in a food processor or blender until thick and smooth. Layer ½ cup of the mushroom mixture in bottom of a baking dish.
2. Mix sliced mushroom stems, brandy, and butter. Fill reserved mushroom caps with mixture; place filled caps in baking dish. Spoon remaining mushroom mixture around mushrooms.
3. Bake at 400°F 20 minutes. Garnish with parsley.

Marinated Pimentos

ABOUT
6 SERVINGS

2 to 3 tablespoons red wine
  vinegar
2 cloves garlic, minced
1 bay leaf
½ teaspoon salt
½ teaspoon pepper
2 tablespoons olive or other
  cooking oil
2 tablespoons chili sauce
2 jars or cans (7 ounces
  each) whole pimentos,
  drained and torn in
  half or in large pieces
1 can anchovy fillets
¼ cup slivered ripe olives
1 tablespoon lemon juice

1. Put the vinegar, garlic, bay leaf, salt, and pepper into a saucepan; simmer 5 minutes.
2. Blend in oil and chili sauce; pour over pimentos. Let stand about 3 hours.
3. To serve, drain pimentos and garnish with anchovy fillets and ripe olives. Drizzle lemon juice over all.

Pickled Zucchini

1 PINT PICKLE

3 to 4 zucchini
5 tablespoons olive oil
2 cloves garlic, quartered
½ teaspoon oregano
¼ teaspoon salt
1 bay leaf
Wine vinegar

1. Wash zucchini and trim off ends. Cut crosswise into ¼-inch slices.
2. Heat 3 tablespoons olive oil in a skillet. Add zucchini and cook slowly until browned. Drain on absorbent paper. Cool and put into a pint screw-top jar.
3. Combine 2 tablespoons oil, garlic, oregano, salt, and bay leaf. Pour into jar. Add enough wine vinegar to cover zucchini.
4. Store, covered, in refrigerator at least 24 hours. Serve cold.

Eggplant Appetizer-Relish

ABOUT
4 CUPS RELISH

¾ cup olive oil
2 cloves garlic, crushed or
  minced
1 large eggplant, sliced,
  pared, and cut in small
  cubes (about 3 cups)
½ cup chopped green
  pepper
½ cup chopped onion
¼ cup finely chopped
  parsley
1 tablespoon sugar
½ teaspoon crushed oregano
¼ teaspoon crushed basil
1 teaspoon seasoned salt
Few grains black pepper
1 cup canned tomato paste
¼ cup water
3 tablespoons red wine
  vinegar
1 can (4 ounces) mushroom
  stems and pieces (do
  not drain)
½ cup very small
  pimento-stuffed olives

1. Heat the oil and garlic in a large, heavy skillet. Add the eggplant, green pepper, onion, and parsley; toss to mix. Cover tightly and cook over low heat about 10 minutes.
2. Meanwhile, blend sugar, oregano, basil, salt, and pepper. Add tomato paste, water, and wine vinegar; mix well. Add to mixture in skillet and stir in remaining ingredients. Cover and cook gently until eggplant is just tender (not mushy).
3. Turn into a bowl and store, covered, in refrigerator overnight to allow flavors to blend.
4. Serve with **crackers.**

Fondues, Pies, and Rarebits

Fish Fondue

6 SERVINGS

12 frozen fish sticks
1 pound mussels (shelled and cooked)
½ pound shrimp (cleaned and cooked)
½ pound lobster meat (cleaned and cooked)
1 quart vegetable (or peanut) oil

Dill mustard sauce
¼ cup beef broth
3 tablespoons dry mustard
2 tablespoons mayonnaise
1 teaspoon dill

Tartar Sauce
¼ cup mayonnaise
½ teaspoon dry mustard
2 tablespoons pickle relish

Chili Sauce
¼ cup ketchup
2 tablespoons chili sauce

Batter
1 cup all-purpose flour
¼ teaspoon salt

Dip
6 eggs, beaten
½ cup milk

1. Heat oil in fondue pot to 375°F.
2. Spear bite-sized fish and dip fish first into egg-milk mixture, then roll in flour batter.
3. Dip fish carefully into hot oil and cook until golden brown, about 30 seconds to 1 minute.
4. Remove from fondue fork, dip in sauce and enjoy.

Buttermilk Fondue

4 TO 6 SERVINGS

1 pound Swiss cheese, shredded (about 4 cups)
3 tablespoons cornstarch
½ teaspoon salt
⅛ teaspoon white pepper
¼ teaspoon dry mustard
2 cups buttermilk
1 clove garlic, split in half
1 loaf dark rye bread, cut into 1-inch cubes

1. Toss cheese with a mixture of cornstarch, salt, pepper, and dry mustard. Set aside.
2. In a fondue saucepan, heat buttermilk with garlic over low heat. When hot, remove garlic and add cheese; stir constantly until cheese is melted.
3. Keep fondue warm over low heat while dipping bread cubes.

Buttermilk Fondue

Swiss Cheese Fondue

ABOUT
6 SERVINGS

1 tablespoon cornstarch
2 tablespoons kirsch
1 clove garlic, halved
2 cups Neuchâtel or other dry white wine
1 pound natural Swiss cheese, shredded (about 4 cups)
Freshly ground black pepper to taste
Ground nutmeg to taste
1 loaf French bread, cut into 1-inch cubes

1. Mix cornstarch and kirsch in a small bowl; set aside.
2. Rub the inside of a nonmetal fondue pot with cut surface of garlic. Pour in wine; place over medium heat until wine is about to simmer (do not boil).
3. Add cheese in small amounts to the hot wine, stirring constantly until cheese is melted. Heat cheese-wine mixture until bubbly.
4. Blend in cornstarch mixture and continue stirring while cooking 5 minutes, or until fondue begins to bubble; add seasoning.
5. Dip bread cubes in fondue. Keep the fondue gently bubbling throughout serving time.

Savory Cheese Custards

4 SERVINGS

1 large yellow onion
¼ teaspoon salt
1½ teaspoons poppy seed
1 cup instant nonfat dry-milk solids
2 cups water
2 teaspoons Worcestershire sauce
2 teaspoons Dijon mustard
¼ teaspoon salt
2 eggs
2 ounces Jarlsberg or Parmesan cheese, finely shredded

1. Bake onion at 400°F until tender when pierced with a fork (about 1½ hours). Let cool. Peel onion and chop finely (about 1½ cups). Mix onion with ¼ teaspoon salt and the poppy seed; spoon mixture into the bottom of 4 ramekins or custard cups.
2. Process dry-milk solids, water, Worcestershire sauce, mustard, ¼ teaspoon salt, and eggs in a food processor or blender until very smooth.
3. Pour mixture into ramekins; sprinkle cheese over mixture. Place ramekins in a shallow baking pan; pour 1 inch boiling water into pan.
4. Bake at 325°F 30 to 40 minutes, or until custard is set and a knife inserted between center and edge comes out clean. Serve warm, or refrigerate and serve cold.

Lombardy Green Tart

6 SERVINGS

1 package (10 ounces) frozen chopped spinach, thawed
2 cups low-fat cottage cheese
1 medium zucchini, minced
2 stalks celery, minced
1 bunch green onions, green part only, minced
2 tablespoons snipped parsley
2 teaspoons snipped fresh or 1 teaspoon dried marjoram leaves
2 teaspoons snipped fresh or 1 teaspoon dried thyme leaves
4 eggs, lightly beaten
½ teaspoon salt
⅛ teaspoon freshly ground pepper
Lettuce leaves

1. Press all liquid from spinach.
2. Combine all ingredients, except lettuce leaves, in a bowl. Mix thoroughly. Spoon mixture into a lightly oiled 9-inch pie plate.
3. Bake at 375°F 45 minutes. Cut into wedges to serve. Serve hot, or refrigerate until chilled and serve on lettuce.

Lombardy Green Salad: Follow recipe for Lombardy Green Tart. Omit eggs, baking, and lettuce. Serve chilled on a bed of **fresh spinach leaves.**

Welsh Rabbit I

⅔ cup lukewarm beer (measured without foam)
1 pound sharp Cheddar cheese (about 4 cups, shredded)
1 tablespoon butter
½ teaspoon Worcestershire sauce
½ teaspoon dry mustard
Few grains cayenne pepper
Crisp toast slices

1. Have beer ready.
2. Shred Cheddar cheese and set aside.
3. Melt butter in top of a double boiler over simmering water.
4. Add cheese all at one time and stir occasionally until cheese begins to melt. Blend in Worcestershire sauce, dry mustard, and cayenne pepper.
5. As soon as cheese begins to melt, add very gradually, stirring constantly, ½ to ⅔ cup beer.
6. As soon as beer is blended in and mixture is smooth, serve immediately over crisp toast slices.

Welsh Rabbit II: Follow recipe for Welsh Rabbit. Substitute **milk** for the beer.

Welsh Rabbit III: Follow recipe for Welsh Rabbit. Substitute **process cheese food** or **sharp process Cheddar cheese** for the sharp Cheddar cheese and **milk** for the beer.

Glorified Welsh Rabbit: Follow recipe for Welsh Rabbit or either variation. Top each serving with a slice of **tomato**, two slices panbroiled **bacon** and a sprig of **parsley.**

Welsh Rabbit in Chafing Dish

6 CUPS
WELSH RABBIT

¼ cup butter
8 cups shredded sharp Cheddar cheese (about 2 pounds)
2 teaspoons Worcestershire sauce
1 teaspoon dry mustard
Few grains cayenne pepper
4 eggs, slightly beaten
1 cup light cream or half-and-half

1. In a chafing dish blazer over simmering water, melt butter. Add cheese and heat, stirring occasionally, until cheese is melted. Mix in Worcestershire sauce, dry mustard, and cayenne pepper.
2. Blend eggs and cream; strain. Mix into melted cheese. Cook until thick, stirring frequently.
3. Garnish with **parsley sprigs.** Serve over toasted **English muffin halves.**

Haitian Rarebit

8 SERVINGS

8 kaiser rolls
16 slices American or Cheddar cheese
½ cup sweet pickle relish
1 cup chopped cooked ham, chicken, beef, or tongue
8 tablespoons butter or margarine, melted

1. Split rolls. On bottom half of each roll, place in the following order: 1 slice cheese, 1 tablespoon sweet pickle relish, 2 tablespoons chopped meat, and another slice cheese. Replace top of roll.
2. Generously brush top and bottom of sandwiches with melted butter.
3. Place rolls in a large skillet over medium heat. Cover with a lid slightly smaller than the skillet and weight it down over the rolls. Brown both sides until cheese melts. Serve immediately.

Cheese Soufflé

8 TO 10 SERVINGS

½ pound sharp process Cheddar cheese (about 2 cups, grated)
6 tablespoons butter or margarine
6 tablespoons all-purpose flour
¾ teaspoon dry mustard
½ teaspoon salt
⅛ teaspoon white pepper
⅛ teaspoon paprika
1½ cups milk
6 egg yolks
6 egg whites

1. Set out a 2-quart casserole; do not grease.
2. Grate Cheddar cheese and set aside.
3. Melt butter or margarine in a saucepan over low heat.
4. Blend in flour, dry mustard, salt, white pepper, and paprika.
5. Heat until mixture bubbles. Remove from heat. Add milk gradually, while stirring constantly.
6. Return to heat and bring rapidly to boiling, stirring constantly; cook 1 to 2 minutes longer. Cool slightly and add the grated cheese all at one time. Stir rapidly until cheese is melted.
7. Beat egg yolks until thick and lemon-colored.
8. Slowly spoon sauce into egg yolks while stirring vigorously.
9. Beat egg whites until rounded peaks are formed and whites do not slide when bowl is partially inverted.
10. Gently spread egg-yolk mixture over beaten egg whites. Carefully fold together until just blended. Turn mixture into casserole. Insert the tip of a spoon 1 inch deep in mixture, 1 to 1½ inches from edge; run a line around mixture. (Center part of soufflé will form a "hat").
11. Bake at 300°F 1 to 1¼ hours, or until a silver knife comes out clean when inserted halfway between center and edge of soufflé.
12. Serve at once, while "top hat" is at its height.

Cheese-Bacon Soufflé: Follow recipe for Cheese Soufflé. Dice and panbroil until crisp 5 slices **bacon.** When bacon is crisped and browned, remove from skillet, set aside on absorbent paper to drain thoroughly. Substitute 3 tablespoons of the reserved **bacon fat** for 3 tablespoons butter or margarine. Fold bacon pieces into egg whites with sauce. Proceed as in recipe.

Salads

Avocados Stuffed with Cauliflower Salad

6 SERVINGS

2 cups very small, crisp raw
  cauliflowerets
1 cup cooked green beans
½ cup sliced ripe olives
¼ cup chopped pimento
¼ cup chopped onion
Oil and Vinegar Dressing
Salt to taste
6 small lettuce leaves
3 large ripe avocados
Lemon wedges

1. Combine all ingredients, except lettuce, avocados, and lemon wedges; stir gently until evenly mixed and coated with dressing.
2. Refrigerate at least 1 hour before serving.
3. When ready to serve, peel, halve, and remove pits from avocados. Place a lettuce leaf on each serving plate; top with avocado half filled with a mound of cauliflower salad. Serve with lemon wedges.

Shrimp and Avocado Salad

ABOUT
8 SERVINGS

1 cup wine vinegar
⅓ cup water
½ cup lemon juice
1 cup salad oil
¼ cup chopped parsley
2 cloves garlic, minced
1 tablespoon salt
¼ teaspoon freshly ground
  black pepper
1 tablespoon sugar
1 teaspoon dry mustard
1 teaspoon thyme, crushed
1 teaspoon oregano, crushed
2 pounds large cooked
  shrimp, peeled and
  deveined
3 small onions, sliced
⅓ cup chopped green pepper
2 ripe avocados, peeled and
  sliced

1. For marinade, combine vinegar, water, lemon juice, oil, parsley, and garlic in a bowl or a screwtop jar. Add a mixture of salt, pepper, sugar, dry mustard, thyme, and oregano; blend thoroughly.
2. Put shrimp, onions, and green pepper into a large shallow dish. Pour marinade over all, cover and refrigerate 8 hours or overnight.
3. About 1 hour before serving, put avocado slices into bowl. Pour enough marinade from shrimp over the avocado to cover completely.
4. To serve, remove avocado slices and shrimp from marinade and arrange on crisp **lettuce** in a large serving bowl.

Pear and Frozen Cheese Salad

8 SERVINGS

4 ounces Roquefort or blue
  cheese (1 cup, crumbled)
½ cup chopped celery
3 ounces (1 package) cream
  cheese
¼ cup mayonnaise
1 tablespoon lemon juice
¼ teaspoon salt
⅛ teaspoon pepper
½ cup chilled whipping
  cream
4 chilled, ripe Bartlett pears
Lemon juice
Curly endive, watercress, or
  other salad greens
French dressing

1. Crumble Roquefort or blue cheese and set aside.
2. Prepare celery and set aside.
3. Beat cream cheese until fluffy.
4. Mix in mayonnaise and lemon juice, and a mixture of salt and pepper, stirring until thoroughly blended after each addition.
5. Stir in the crumbled cheese and chopped celery. Set mixture aside.
6. Using a chilled bowl and beater, beat whipping cream until cream is of medium consistency (piles softly).
7. Gently fold into cheese mixture. Turn into a chilled refrigerator tray. Put into freezing compartment of refrigerator and freeze until cheese mixture is firm.
8. When ready to serve, cut frozen cheese into 1-inch cubes.

(continued)

9. *For Bartlett Pear Salad* – Rinse well, cut into halves and core Bartlett pears.
10. Brush cut sides of pears with lemon juice.
11. Place salad greens on each of 8 chilled salad plates.
12. Put one pear half, cut side up, on each plate. Place two or three frozen Roquefort or blue cheese cubes in hollow of each pear half. Or arrange greens, pear halves and cheese cubes on a large chilled serving plate.
13. Serve immediately with French dressing.

Smorgasbord Pear Salads

12 SALADS

6 fresh Bartlett pears
Shrimp Filling
Zippy Cheese Filling
Celery-Olive Filling
Salad Greens

1. Halve and core pears. Fill 4 halves with Shrimp Filling, 4 with Zippy Cheese Filling, and 4 with Celery-Olive Filling.
2. Arrange filled pear halves on salad greens in a large shallow bowl or on a serving platter.

Shrimp Filling: Chop **1 cup cooked deveined shrimp** and combine with **¼ cup chopped celery, 2 tablespoons chopped parsley, 2 teaspoons instant minced onion, ½ teaspoon salt,** and **⅓ cup mayonnaise.**

Zippy Cheese Filling: Combine **1 cup cottage cheese, 1 tablespoon drained capers,** and **1 tablespoon chopped pimento-stuffed olives.**

Celery-Olive Filling: Combine in a small bowl **1 cup cooked sliced celery, ¼ cup ripe olives,** cut in wedges, and **1 tablespoon diced pimento.** Put into a jar with a lid **⅓ cup salad oil, 2 tablespoons vinegar, ½ teaspoon salt,** and **1½ teaspoons sugar;** cover and shake to blend. Pour over celery mixture. Let marinate 2 hours, stirring occasionally.

Smogasbord Pear Salads

Cold Soups

Gazpacho

4 SERVINGS

2 cans (6 ounces each)
  seasoned tomato juice
½ cucumber, coarsely sliced
1 tomato, quartered
¼ cup vinegar
¼ cup salad oil
1 tablespoon sugar
1 can or bottle (25.6 ounces)
  seasoned tomato juice
½ cucumber, chopped
1 tomato, chopped
1 small onion, chopped
Minced parsley
Chopped hard-cooked egg
Chopped cucumber
Croutons

1. Pour the 12 ounces tomato juice into an electric blender. Add sliced cucumber, tomato, vinegar, oil, and sugar; blend.
2. Serve with bowls of parsley, hard-cooked egg, cucumber, and croutons.

Gazpacho Garden Soup

6 SERVINGS

3 large tomatoes, chopped
1 clove garlic, crushed
1 small cucumber, chopped
1 green pepper, chopped
½ cup sliced green onions
¼ cup chopped onion
¼ cup minced parsley
1 teaspoon crushed rosemary
¼ teaspoon crushed basil
½ teaspoon salt
¼ cup olive oil
¼ cup salad oil
2 tablespoons lemon juice
2 cups chicken broth or 3
  chicken bouillon cubes
  dissolved in 2 cups boiling
  water, then cooled

1. Combine all ingredients except chicken broth in a large bowl. Toss gently.
2. Stir in chicken broth; chill.
3. Serve in chilled bowls with garnishes suggested in Gazpacho.

Sailor's Borsch

ABOUT
2 QUARTS
SOUP

1 can (46 ounces) tomato
  juice
1 tablespoon beef stock base
1 teaspoon salt
1 can or jar (16 ounces)
  sliced beets
⅓ cup coarsely chopped
  parsley
2 tablespoons red wine
  vinegar
1 carton (8 ounces) plain
  yogurt

1. Heat 1 cup tomato juice, beef stock base, and salt in a saucepan. Stir until beef stock base and salt are dissolved.
2. Combine 1 cup tomato juice with beets and liquid, parsley, and vinegar in an electric blender or bowl; blend or beat until beets are finely chopped. Combine both mixtures with remaining tomato juice. Chill.
3. Top each serving with a dollop of yogurt.

Note: Borsch may be served hot. Yogurt may be stirred in just before serving, if desired.

Vichyssoise (Chilled Leek and Potato Soup)

8 SERVINGS

4 to 6 leeks
2 tablespoons butter or
  margarine
4 potatoes, pared and sliced
1 quart chicken broth or 6
  chicken bouillon cubes
  dissolved in 1 quart
  boiling water
1 cup half-and-half
1 cup chilled whipping
  cream
Snipped chives

1. Finely slice the white part and about an inch of the green part of each leek to measure about 1 cup.
2. Sauté leeks in butter in a heavy saucepan. Stir in potatoes and broth; bring to boiling. Simmer 40 minutes, or until potatoes are tender.
3. Sieve the cooked vegetables or blend until smooth in an electric blender. Mix in half-and-half; chill thoroughly.
4. Just before serving, stir in whipping cream. Garnish with chives.

Cucumber Soup, Danish Style

6 SERVINGS

2 medium cucumbers, pared
2 tablespoons butter
1 medium leek, sliced
2 bay leaves
1 tablespoon flour
1 teaspoon salt
3 cups chicken broth
1 medium cucumber, pared
  and grated (discard seeds)
1 cup chilled light cream
Juice of ½ lemon

1. Slice 2 cucumbers; cook slowly in butter with the leek and bay leaves until tender but not brown. Stir in the flour and salt. Heat until bubbly.
2. Stir in the broth. Simmer 20 to 30 minutes. Press mixture through a sieve and chill.
3. Add grated cucumber, cream, lemon juice, and a bit of **chopped fresh dill.** Correct seasoning.
4. Serve in chilled cups with a dollop of **dairy sour cream** on top of each.

Norwegian Fruit Soup

ABOUT
3½ CUPS
SOUP

1 quart water
2 tablespoons rice
½ cup finely chopped apple
1 cup pitted dark sweet
  cherries and juice
½ cup red raspberry fruit
  syrup
¼ cup lemon juice
2-inch piece stick cinnamon
1 tablespoon cold water
1 teaspoon cornstarch

1. Bring 1 quart water to boiling in a deep saucepan.
2. Add 2 tablespoons rice to water so boiling will not stop. Boil rapidly, uncovered, 15 to 20 minutes, or until a kernel is entirely soft when pressed between fingers. Drain rice, reserving liquid.
3. Rinse and finely chop enough apple to yield ½ cup.
4. Put cherries into a bowl.
5. Add fruit syrup and lemon juice.
6. Return the rice water to the saucepan. Add the apple and cinnamon stick.
7. Cook over medium heat 4 to 5 minutes, or until apple is tender. Add the drained rice and the cherry mixture. Remove the cinnamon. Simmer 5 minutes.
8. Blend together cold water and cornstarch to form a smooth paste.
9. Blend cornstarch mixture into soup. Bring to boiling. Continue to cook 3 to 5 minutes. Cool soup slightly.
10. Serve soup warm or cold. If serving soup cold, garnish with **whipped cream.**

Raisin Fruit Soup: Follow recipe for Norwegian Fruit Soup. Omit cherries. Increase red raspberry syrup to 1 cup. Add to the syrup mixture 1 cup (about 5 ounces) dark seedless **raisins.**

Appetizers from the Microwave Oven

Microwave cooking lets you mingle with your guests while you amaze them with the wide variety of tempting nibbles you have prepared with a minimum of last-minute fuss. Many of the appetizers can be prepared the night before and just popped into the microwave oven for last-minute heating as the guests arrive.

For greater convenience, heat the appetizers right on a microwave-safe serving plate. Remember to arrange individual appetizers in a circle for more even heating. If desired, place a bowl of cold snack food in the center of the serving plate. Or for a warm treat, heat a bowl of your favorite salted nuts for a few minutes for quick and easy munching.

Hot Tuna Canapés

1 can (6½ or 7 ounces) tuna
¼ cup mayonnaise
1 tablespoon ketchup
¼ teaspoon salt
Few grains cayenne pepper
2 teaspoons finely chopped
 onion
¼ teaspoon Worcestershire
 sauce
1 cucumber
Paprika (optional)
48 Melba toast rounds
12 pimento-stuffed olives,
 sliced

1. Drain and flake tuna. Add mayonnaise, ketchup, salt, cayenne pepper, onion and Worcestershire sauce.
2. Pare cucumber and slice paper-thin (if desired, sprinkle with paprika).
3. For each canapé, place cucumber slice on toast round, pile tuna mixture in center and top with olive slice.
4. Put 8 canapés in circle on 6 individual paper plates. For each plate, cook uncovered in microwave oven 30 to 60 seconds.

Greek Meatballs

50 TO 60
MEATBALLS

1 pound ground lamb
1 egg
⅓ cup cracker crumbs
⅓ cup soy sauce
½ cup water
¼ teaspoon ginger
¼ teaspoon garlic powder
⅛ teaspoon cumin
½ cup almonds or slivered
  almonds

1. In a medium mixing bowl, blend lamb, egg, and cracker crumbs. Add soy sauce, water, ginger, garlic powder, cumin, and pinenuts. Mix thoroughly. Shape in 1-inch meatballs.
2. Arrange 10 meatballs in a circle in a 9-inch glass pie plate. Cook, covered, 3 to 4 minutes, rotating dish one-quarter turn halfway through cooking time. Cook longer if needed.
3. Serve hot on wooden picks.

Appetizer Kabobs

40 APPETIZERS

8 large precooked smoked
  sausage links
1 can (16 ounces) pineapple
  chunks, drained
1 tablespoon brown sugar
2 tablespoons soy sauce
1 tablespoon vinegar

1. Arrange sausage evenly around edge of roasting rack set in a glass dish or directly on glass plate and cook 2 to 3 minutes, rotating dish one-quarter turn halfway through cooking time. Drain sausage and cut each sausage link into 5 pieces.
2. Make kabobs, using 1 sausage piece and 1 pineapple chunk threaded on a round wooden pick. Arrange evenly in a large shallow dish.
3. In a 1-cup glass measure, blend brown sugar, soy sauce, and vinegar and pour over kabobs. Refrigerate 1 or 2 hours until serving time.
4. Arrange 20 kabobs on a large glass plate and cook 2 to 3 minutes, rotating dish one-quarter turn and spooning sauce over top halfway through cooking time.
5. Cook additional kabobs as needed. Serve warm.

Chicken-Stuffed Mushrooms

30 APPETIZERS

30 fresh medium mushrooms
1 can (4½ ounces) chicken
  spread
½ teaspoon seasoned salt
⅛ teaspoon pepper
1 tablespoon chopped parsley
½ cup chopped walnuts

1. Wash mushrooms quickly under cold water. Remove stems, and drain both stems and caps on paper towel.
2. In a small mixing bowl, blend chicken spread, seasoned salt, pepper, parsley, and walnuts. Stuff mushrooms; place stems in filling and secure with wooden pick.
3. Arrange mushrooms on a glass pie plate and cook, covered with waxed paper, 6 to 8 minutes, rotating dish one-quarter turn halfway through cooking time. Serve hot.

Conventional oven: Bake at 350°F 20 minutes.

On opposite page:
Greek Meatballs
Appetizer Kabobs
Chicken - Stuffed Mushrooms

Spicy Beef Dip

ABOUT
3 CUPS DIP

1 pound ground beef
½ cup chopped onion
1 clove garlic, minced
1 can (8 ounces) tomato
  sauce
¼ cup ketchup
¾ teaspoon oregano,
  crushed
1 teaspoon sugar
1 package (3 ounces) cream
  cheese
⅓ cup grated Parmesan
  cheese

1. In a 1½-quart glass casserole, sauté ground beef, onion, and garlic 4 to 6 minutes, stirring twice.
2. Spoon off excess fat. Stir in tomato sauce, ketchup, oregano, and sugar.
3. Cover and cook 5 to 6 minutes, stirring twice.
4. Add cream cheese and Parmesan cheese, and stir until cream cheese has melted. Serve warm.

Sweet-and-Sour Wiener Fondue

60 TO 70
APPETIZERS

1 jar (5 ounces) currant
  jelly
½ cup prepared mustard
1 pound wieners, cut in
  bite-size pieces

1. In a small glass mixing bowl, combine jelly and mustard. Cook 2 minutes, stirring halfway through cooking time.
2. Add wieners and cook 3 to 4 minutes, stirring halfway through cooking time
3. Serve warm.

Chicken Livers and Mushrooms

4 TO 6
SERVINGS

1 to 1½ pounds chicken
  livers
½ pound fresh mushrooms,
  thinly sliced
¼ cup grated onion
2 tablespoons chopped
  parsley
¾ teaspoon salt
½ teaspoon pepper
½ cup burgundy
¼ cup butter
6 slices toast or 3 English
  muffins, split and toasted

1. Dice livers coarsely. Combine with mushrooms, onion, parsley, salt, pepper, and wine in a large plastic bag. Marinate in refrigerator overnight.
2. In a 2-quart glass casserole, heat butter 30 to 45 seconds. Add chicken-liver mixture.
3. Cook, uncovered, 6 to 8 minutes, stirring every 2 minutes. Cover casserole and cook 3 to 4 minutes more.
4. Spoon onto toasted bread or muffins arranged on serving platter.

Quick Cheese Fondue

2 CUPS
FONDUE

1 can (10½ ounces) con-
  densed Cheddar cheese
  soup
⅓ cup milk
¼ teaspoon garlic powder
¼ teaspoon nutmeg
1½ cups shredded Swiss
  cheese

1. In a 4-cup glass measure, blend soup and milk; cook 3 to 4 minutes, stirring halfway through cooking time.
2. Add garlic powder and nutmeg; stir to blend. Blend in cheese.
3. Cook 2 to 3 minutes, stirring every minute, until cheese is melted.
4. Serve immediately while warm.

Index

Acra, 32
Anchovy
  Butter, 22
  Fillets, 50
Appetizer(s)
  Eggplant, 20
  Hot Shrimp, 55
  Kabobs, 76
  Peekaboo, 27
  Puffs, 18
  -Relish, Eggplant, 65
  Tray, Fresh Sweet
    Cherry, 34
Artichoke Plate, Chilled, 60
Artichokes, George's
  Greek Style, 61
Aspic, Beermato, 38
Aspic, Tomato, 37
Avocado
  -Pineapple Filling, 15
  Rye Rounds, 14
  Sandwiches on Sour
    Dough, 12
  Stuffed With Cauliflower
    Salad, 71
  Voisin, 52

Barbecued Lamb Innards, 29
Basic Dinner Crêpes, 17
Béarnaise Sauce, Mock, 60
Beermato Aspic, 38
Blue Cheese in a Melon, 23
Borsch, Sailor's 73
Broiled Fish Quenelles, 50
Butter(s)
  Anchovy, 22
  Canapé, 22
  Cheese, 22
  Chili, 22
  Dried Beef, 22
  Egg, 22
  Ham, 22
  Horseradish, 22
  Mustard, 22
  Olive, 22
  Onion-Chive, 22
  Pimiento, 22
  Shrimp, 22
Buttermilk Fondue, 66

Calf, Lamb, or Chicken Livers,
  Fried, 29
Canapés
  Butters, 22
  Curried Cheese, 9
  Daisy, 10
  Half-and-half, 10

Hot Tuna, 75
Marrow, 10
Olive, 10
Sardine, 9
Shrimp, 9
Suggestions, 8
Tomato-and-Egg, 10
Wine-Cheese, 9
Carrots, Pickled, 62
Celery-Olive Filling, 72
Celery-Rings, Stuffed, 62
Cheddar-Sausage Rolls, 56
Cheese
  -Bacon Soufflé, 70
  Butter, 22
  Custard, Savory, 68
  Fried, 26
  Mousse, 40
  Roll, Fried, 35
  -Shrimp Filling, 15
  Soufflé, 70
Chicken
  Fritters Guadeloupe, 30
  Livers and Mushrooms, 78
  Liver Spread, 20
  Mousse Amandine, 40
  -Mushroom Sandwiches, 12
  Stock, 43
  -Stuffed Mushrooms, 76
  Tantalizers in Cherry
    Sauce, 56
  Terrines, Individual, 42
  Wings, Oriental, 56
Chili
  Butter, 22
  con Queso Dip, 24
  -Nut Log, 35
  Pinwheels, 35
  Turnovers, 35
Chilled Artichoke Plate, 60
Clam and Walnut Stuffed
  Mushrooms, 26
Clear Glaze, 9
Cocktail Frank Wrap-Ups, 34
Cocktail Meatballs, 28
Corn Fritters, 31
Court Bouillon for Fish and
  Shellfish, 21
Crab Meat
  and Bean Sprouts with
    Omelet Strips, 51
  in Rolls, 14
  Newburg Appetizer, 52
  Quiche, 26
Crackers, Crisp Cheese, 14
Cranberry-Cheese
  Frosting, 15
Creamy Corn Dip, 23
Creamy Shrimp Dip, 23
Crêpes, Basic Dinner, 17
Crêpes, Wafer, 17
Crisp Cheese Crackers, 14
Crusty Roll Tempters, 15

Cucumber Sauce, 43
Cucumber Soup, Danish
  Style, 74
Curried Cheese Canapés, 9

Daisy Canapés, 10
Deviled Ham-Peanut Butter
  Filling, 15
Dill Pickles, 62
Dip
  Creamy Corn, 23
  Creamy Shrimp, 23
  Spicy Beef, 78
  Tangy Cheese, 24
Dried Beef Butter, 22

Egg-Bacon Filling, 15
Egg Butter, 22
Eggplant
  Appetizer, 20
  Appetizer-Relish, 65
  Fritters, 31
Egg Rolls, 30
Eggs with Anchovies, 51
Empanadas, 28

Fabulous Cheese Mousse, 39
Feet in Aspic, 39
Feta Cheese Triangles, 25
Filling
  Avocado-Pineapple, 15
  Celery-Olive, 72
  Cheese-Shrimp, 15
  Deviled Ham-Peanut
    Butter, 15
  Egg-Bacon, 15
  Shrimp, 72
  Zippy Cheese, 72
Fish
  Balls, 48
  Fondue, 66
  Quenelles, Broiled, 50
Flybanes, 64
Fondue
  Buttermilk, 66
  Fish, 66
  Quick Cheese, 78
  Sweet-and-Sour Wiener
    Fondue, 78
  Swiss Cheese, 68
Fresh Mushrooms in Sour
  Cream, 32
Fresh Sweet Cherry Appetizer
  Tray, 34
Fried
  Calf, Lamb, or Chicken
    Livers, 29
  Cheese, 26
  Cheese Roll, 35
Fritters
  Chicken, 30
  Corn, 31
  Eggplant, 31

Frosting, Cranberry-
  Cheese, 15
Fruit Soup, Norwegian, 74
Fruit Soup, Raisin, 74

Gazpacho, 73
Gazpacho Garden Soup, 73
Gefillte Fish, 48
George's Greek-Style
  Artichokes, 61
German Beer Cheese, 37
Glaze, Clear, 9
Glorified Welsh Rabbit, 69
Gourmet Gouda Spread, 18
Grape Leaves, Stuffed, 61
Greek Meatballs, 76
Guacamole, 21

Haitian Rarebit, 69
Half-and-Half Canapés, 10
Ham and Egg Rolls, 56
Ham Butter, 22
Ham Loaf en Brioche, 16
ham Mousse, 40
Hawaiian Sandwiches, 12
Herbed Stuffed
  Mushrooms, 64
Herring, Pickled, 50
Hollandaise Sauce, Mock, 60
Horseradish, 49
Horseradish Butter, 22
Hot Crab Spread, 19
Hot Shrimp Appetizer, 55
Hot Tuna Canapés, 75

Individual Chicken
  Terrines, 42

Jellied Mélange, 39

Kabobs
  Appetizer, 76
  Lamb, 59

Lamb Innards, Barbecued, 29
Lamb Kabobs, 59
Liver-Bologna Spread, 20
Liver Pâté, 44
Lombardy Green Salad, 68
Lombardy Green Tart, 68
Low-Fat Yogurt, 43

Marinated Pimentos, 65
Marrow Canapés, 10
Mayonnaise, Mock, 60
Meatballs
  Cocktail, 28
  Greek, 76
  Swedish, 58
Mock
  Béarnaise Sauce, 60
  Hollandaise Sauce, 60
  Mayonnaise, 60

Mold
Mushroom Cheese, 36
Mustard Relish, 37
Mosaic Sandwiches, 12
Mousse
Amandine, Chicken, 40
Cheese, 40
Fabulous Cheese 39
Ham, 40
Mushroom(s)
à la Grecque, 63
Cheese Mold, 36
Chicken-Stuffed, 76
Clam and Walnut
Stuffed, 26
Fresh in Sour Cream, 32
Herbed Stuffed, 64
Pickled, 63
Mustard Butter, 22
Mustard Relish Mold, 37

Nippy Beef Spread, 17
Norwegian Fruit Soup, 74

Octopus, Pickled, 55
Olive Butter, 22
Olive Canapés, 10
Olive Pinwheels, 14
Onion-Chive Butter, 22
Oriental Chicken Wings, 56
Oysters Rockefeller, 55

Party Spread, 17
Pâté
à la Maison, 44
Liver, 44
Pork, 44
Pear and Frozen Cheese
Salad, 71
Peekaboo Appetizers, 27

Peppery Peanut Butter and
Coconut Sandwiches, 11
Pickled
Carrots, 62
Herring, 50
Mushrooms, 63
Octopus, 55
Shrimp, 54
Watermelon Rind, 62
Zucchini, 65
Pickles, Dill, 62
Pimentos, Marinated, 65
Pimiento Butter, 22
Pinwheels
Chili, 35
Olive, 14
Pork Pâté, 44
Puff Shrimp with Orange
Ginger Sauce, 27

Quiche, Crab Meat, 26
Quick Cheese Fondue, 78

Raisin Fruit Soup, 74
Rarebit, Haitian, 69
Rémoulade with Scallops, 27
Rolls, Cheddar-Sausage, 56
Russian Salmon Mound, 46

Sailor's Borsch, 73
Salad, Lombardy, Green, 68
Salmon Mound, Russian, 46
Sandwiches
Avocado, 12
Chicken-Mushroom, 12
Hawaiian, 12
Mosaic, 12
Peppery Peanut Butter and
Coconut, 11
Sandwich Log, Yule, 15

Sardine Canapés, 9
Sardine Spread, 18
Sauce, Cucumber, 43
Savory Cheese Custard, 68
Scallops, Rémoulade with, 27
Seviche, 51
Shrimp
and Avocado Salad, 71
Butter, 22
Canapés, 9
Cocktail, 54
Dunk, 54
Filling, 72
Mélange, 39
Paste à la Creole, 21
Pickled, 54
Spread, 18
with Orange Ginger Sauce,
Puff, 27
Smorgasbord Pear Salads, 72
Soufflé, Cheese, 70
Soufflé, Cheese-Bacon, 70
Soup, Cucumber, 74
Spicy Beef Dip, 78
Spicy Steak Tartare, 58
Spread
Gourmet Gouda, 18
Hot Crab, 19
Liver-Bologna, 20
Nippy Beef, 17
Party, 17
Sardine, 18
Shrimp, 18
Spring Cottage Cheese, 20
Spring Cottage Cheese
Spread, 20
Steak Tartare, Spicy, 58
Steak Tartare with
Vegetables, 57
Stock, Chicken, 43

Stuffed Celery Rings, 62
Stuffed Grape Leaves, 61
Swedish Meat Balls, 58
Sweet-and-Sour Wiener
Fondue, 78
Swiss Cheese Fondue, 68

Tangerine Yakatori, 29
Tangy Cheese Dip, 24
Tart, Lombardy Green, 68
Teriyaki, 57
Toast, Tomato, 32
Tomato
-and-Egg Canapés, 10
Aspic, 37
Sandwich Hors
d'Oeuvres, 11
Toast, 32
Tuna in a Cucumber, 11
Turnovers, Chili, 35

Veal Picks, 59
Vegetable Mélange with
Mustard Sauce, 64
Vichissoise, 74

Wafer Crêpes, 17
Watermelon Rind, Picled, 62
Welsh Rabbit, 69
Glorified, 69
in Chafing Dish, 69
Wine-Cheese Canapés, 9

Yakatori, Tangerine, 29
Yogurt, Low-Fat, 43
Yule Sandwich Log, 15

Zippy Cheese Filling, 72
Zucchini, Pickled, 65